First published in Great Britain in 2026 by Hamlyn, an imprint of
Octopus Publishing Group Ltd
Carmelite House
50 Victoria Embankment
London EC4Y 0DZ
www.octopusbooks.co.uk

An Hachette UK Company
www.hachette.co.uk

The authorized representative in the EEA is Hachette Ireland, 8 Castlecourt Centre, Dublin 15, D15 XTP3, Ireland (email: info@hbgi.ie)

Distributed in the US by
Hachette Book Group
1290 Avenue of the Americas,
4th and 5th Floors
New York, NY 10104

Distributed in Canada by
Canadian Manda Group
664 Annette St., Toronto,
Ontario, Canada M6S 2C8

ISBN: 978-0-60064-062-2
eISBN: 978-0-60064-063-9

A CIP catalogue record for this book is available from the British Library.

Printed and bound in Great Britain

10 9 8 7 6 5 4 3 2 1

Publisher: Lucy Pessell
Senior Editor: Katie Button
Senior Designer: Alicia House
Assistant Editor: Samina Rahman
Production Manager: Caroline Alberti
Illustrator: Mauro Mazzara

FSC
www.fsc.org
MIX
Paper | Supporting responsible forestry
FSC® C104740

This FSC® label means that materials used for the product have been responsibly sourced.

UNOFFICIAL
AND UNAUTHORISED

A TASTE OF THORNS AND ROSES

A ROMANTASY COOKBOOK

hamlyn

CONTENTS

INTRODUCTION

We all know there's nothing better than getting lost in a red-hot romance in fantastical worlds where the usual rules don't apply. Magical forces can make *anything* happen and what's not to like about that?

From the desert of Zilvaren to the provinces of Navarre, fierce adventuresses are straining in their pursuit of justice, growing into power, expertise and strategic competence while their smoking-hot mates give them a dangerous dose of complex vulnerability and the occasional very pleasurable bite.

And at the end of a hard day's lesson or a hard night's ride, there's the food. For us mortals, all that sumptuous, sensory, sensual culinary detail is magic in itself. Who doesn't want to taste freshly landed spices on the banks of the Velaris' sapphire Sidra River, or smell smoky-rich pasta sauce in a nineteenth-century Sicilian trattoria, or watch a god-tier brooding rival lick dripping honey from his finger…? In worlds like Prythian or Callipolis, Solis or the Martial Empire, food is about enchantment, death or survival, safety, trust or seduction, telling us as much about hierarchies and histories as individual lives and moods. A whole roast goose on a golden platter or a gifted truth tonic in a carved wooden mug can take us to very different dimensions, from the decadence of Renaissance vampire courts to a humble forager's cottage in erratic faerie time. No wonder we can't get enough.

Not knowing whether the offer of a buttery pastry comes with a lifetime of protection or a hundred years' hard service to a wicked demon overlord certainly raises the stakes. But sharing food with friends, or sealing your mating bond with a meal, is a universally understood and deeply human language of care and connection. Inspired by magical romance and fantastical realms, this collection of recipes sets out in that spirit: to bring you delicious dishes that are comforting and restorative, beautiful to look at and perfect for sharing in any world you choose.

MORNING FARE & FLIGHT BITES

Whether choosing your eternal partner or the next move in an apocalyptic war, nobody thinks clearly on an empty stomach. It's hard work, all that battling evil forces, laying siege on demon ground and trying not to fall for morally questionable fae warriors – and you certainly won't last the 18-hour journey from Basgiath to Aretia on dragonback without *something* to keep you going.

But daybreak is also the window between light and darkness, when nighttime fantasy and illusion give way to everyday realities. Morning can be a time for new beginnings, quiet contemplation and, sometimes, unexpected intimacy... Is a grumbling belly really the right soundtrack for sunrise flights and early-morning sparring sessions?

You might be feeding a significant other, but feeding yourself is the kind of meaningful self-care all heroines need too – either way, breakfast should give you the slow-burning fuel you need for the day ahead, whatever it has in store.

With that in mind, this section is all about magical no-fuss breakfasts and hearty brunchtime bites that are filling, delicious and just spicy enough to get everyone awake and ready for action.

FORAGER WOODLAND TOAST

As forest roamers like Tobias Finch and Feyre Archeron will tell you, there's nothing quite like the cosy smell of buttery garlic and earthy mushrooms sizzling in a pan. This simple, comforting breakfast is full of wildwood goodness to set you up for the day. Goes well with sausages, if you like.

Serves 4
Preparation time 10 minutes | Cooking time 5 minutes

25 g (1 oz) butter
3 tablespoons extra virgin olive oil, plus extra to serve
750 g (1½ lb) mixed mushrooms, such as oyster, shiitake, flat and button, trimmed and sliced
2 garlic cloves, crushed
1 tablespoon chopped thyme
grated zest and juice of 1 lemon
2 tablespoons chopped parsley
4 slices of sourdough bread
100 g (3½ oz) mixed salad leaves
salt and black pepper
fresh Parmesan cheese shavings, to serve

Melt the butter with the oil in a large frying pan (skillet). As soon as the butter stops foaming, add the mushrooms, garlic, thyme, lemon zest and salt and pepper and cook over a medium heat, stirring, for 4–5 minutes until tender. Scatter over the parsley and squeeze over a little lemon juice.

Meanwhile, toast the bread, then arrange it on serving plates. Top the sourdough toast with an equal quantity of the salad leaves and mushrooms, and drizzle over a little more oil and the lemon juice. Scatter with Parmesan shavings and serve immediately.

DRAGONFIRED RÖSTI & FRAZZLED EGGS (V)

Scorched by dragonfire or cooked in a pan, few things go together so well as golden potato rösti and sticky fried eggs. With even bigger 'crispy on the outside, tender in the middle' vibes than our favourite brooding antiheroes, this tasty, filling combo is the perfect start to a hard day's slaying. Add bacon for a meaty boost, or spice it up with a dash of hot sauce.

Serves 4

Preparation time 15 minutes | Cooking time 15 minutes

750 g (1½ lb) Desiree (Yukon Gold) potatoes, peeled
1 onion, thinly sliced
2 teaspoons chopped rosemary
4 tablespoons olive oil
4 large eggs
salt and black pepper
chopped parsley, to garnish

Using a box grater, coarsely grate the potatoes. Wrap in a clean tea towel (dish towel) and squeeze out the excess liquid over the sink. Transfer to a bowl and stir in the onion, rosemary and salt and pepper.

Heat half the oil in a large frying pan (skillet). Divide the potato mixture into quarters and spoon into 4 x 12 cm (5 inch) mounds in the pan, pressing down to form patties. Cook over a medium heat for 5 minutes on each side, transfer to serving plates and keep warm in a moderate oven.

Heat the remaining oil in the frying pan for about 1 minute until very hot, add the eggs, 2 at a time, and fry until the whites are bubbly and crisp looking. Serve the eggs on the rösti, garnished with chopped parsley.

BAKED EGGS FOR REBELS (V)

Whether you're starting a revolution, infiltrating a dodgy fae court or just trying not to catch feelings, fighting oppressive systems takes a *lot* of energy. This moreish dish of warm, smoky peppers, spicy tomatoes and creamy baked eggs is ideal fuel for another day of resistance. Mop up the sauces with crusty bread, or top with crumbled black pudding (blood sausage) for meaty tang.

Serves 4

Preparation time 10 minutes | Cooking time 25 minutes

2 tablespoons olive oil
1 onion, finely chopped
2 garlic cloves, crushed
1 teaspoon sweet smoked paprika
1 thyme sprig
2 x 400 g (13 oz) cans chopped tomatoes
200 ml (7 fl oz) water
4 eggs
salt and black pepper
chopped parsley, to garnish

Heat the oil in a large, deep frying pan (skillet), add the onion and cook for 5 minutes until softened. Stir in the garlic and paprika and cook for a further 30 seconds.

Add the thyme sprig, tomatoes and the measurement water, then season with salt and pepper. Bring to the boil, then reduce the heat and simmer for 10 minutes until rich and thickened.

Make 4 small pockets in the tomato sauce, then break an egg into each one. Cover the pan with foil and simmer for about 5 minutes until the egg whites are cooked through. Serve scattered with chopped parsley.

AVALON BLUFF STICKY MORNING PANCAKES (V)

When you realize your one-time rival is your all-time love, you need a breakfast that's syrupy-sweet and perfect for sharing – and these stacked soft pancakes drizzled with rich blueberry sauce are one such wholesome treat. Serve with Greek-style yogurt or crème fraîche, or bacon for savoury contrast.

Serves 4–6

Preparation time 10 minutes | Cooking time 20 minutes

15 g (½ oz) butter
150 g (5 oz) self-raising (self-rising) flour
1 teaspoon bicarbonate of soda (baking soda)
40 g (1½ oz) caster (superfine) sugar
1 egg, beaten
350 ml (12 fl oz) buttermilk
icing (confectioners') sugar, for dusting
Greek-style yogurt or crème fraîche, to serve

FOR THE BLUEBERRY SAUCE

250 g (8 oz) fresh blueberries
2 tablespoons clear honey
dash of lemon juice

Heat the blueberries with the honey and lemon juice in a small saucepan over a low heat for about 3 minutes until they release their juices. Keep warm.

Melt the butter in a separate small saucepan. Sift the flour and bicarbonate of soda (baking soda) into a bowl and stir in the caster (superfine) sugar. Beat the egg and buttermilk together in a separate bowl or jug (pitcher), then gradually whisk into the dry ingredients with the melted butter to make a smooth batter.

Heat a nonstick frying pan (skillet) until hot. Drop in large spoonfuls of the batter and cook over a high heat for 3 minutes until bubbles appear on the surface. Flip the pancakes over and cook for a further minute. Remove and keep warm in a moderate oven. Repeat with the remaining batter.

Serve the pancakes topped with the blueberry sauce and a dusting of icing (confectioners') sugar and a dollop of yoghurt or crème fraîche.

HOT PEACH & HONEY PANCAKES (V)

If it feels like you've waited hundreds of years to breakfast with that enigmatic figure who keeps popping up in your life, then when you finally do manage to connect, make sure it's over something luscious and sweet like these decadent pancakes topped with peaches and honey.

Makes 8

Preparation time 10 minutes | Cooking time 20 minutes

3 small ripe peaches
1 teaspoon ground cinnamon
6 tablespoons clear honey
125 g (4 oz) self-raising (self-rising) flour
2 tablespoons golden caster (superfine) sugar
1 egg
150 ml (¼ pint) milk
little oil, for greasing

Halve and stone the peaches. Roughly chop 1 of them and set it aside, then cut the remaining 2 into wedges and toss with a small pinch of the ground cinnamon and all the honey in a small bowl and set aside.

Sift the flour and remaining cinnamon into a bowl and add the sugar. Make a well in the centre and set aside. Beat the egg and milk together well in a jug (pitcher), then pour into the centre of the flour mixture. Mix quickly and as lightly as possible to make a batter the consistency of thick cream. Stir in the chopped peaches.

Lightly oil a heavy-based frying pan (skillet) or flat griddle pan. Drop heaped tablespoons of the batter on to the pan surface and cook over a steady, moderate heat for 1–2 minutes until bubbles rise to the surface and burst. Turn the pancake over and cook for a further 1–2 minutes. Remove from the pan and keep warm while making the remaining pancakes.

Serve the pancakes warm, with a large spoonful of the peach and honey mixture over the top of each.

THE

SUN QUEEN'S MORNING DELIGHT (V)

Bring the taste of summer straight to your lips with creamy ricotta, tangy sweet fruit and lashings of honey – a breakfast fit for a queen, whether fearless fae or mighty mortal. Add sourdough toast for carbs, or toasted nuts for extra protein.

Serves 4
Preparation time 10 minutes

125 g (4 oz) fresh raspberries
2 teaspoons rosewater
250 g (8 oz) ricotta cheese
250 g (8 oz) fresh mixed summer berries
2 tablespoons clear honey with honeycomb
2 tablespoons pumpkin seeds, toasted
pinch of ground cinnamon

Rub the raspberries through a fine nylon sieve (strainer) to purée and remove the pips, then mix with the rosewater. Alternatively, put the raspberries and rosewater in a food processor or blender and process to a purée, then sieve to remove the pips.

Slice the ricotta into wedges and arrange on serving plates with the berries. Drizzle over the honey and the raspberry purée, adding a little honeycomb, and serve scattered with the pumpkin seeds and cinnamon.

BRENNAN'S HONEYED BISCUITS (V)

In *Fourth Wing*, Brennan Sorrengail was on to a good thing with his favourite breakfast, because freshly baked biscuits (or scones, outside of Navarre) slathered in butter and honey are the ultimate mending treat. Eat these moist, fluffy mounds warm from the oven, or save them for a mid-morning pick-me-up.

Makes about 10

Preparation time 10 minutes | Cooking time 10 minutes

250 g (8 oz) plain (all-purpose) flour
1 teaspoon cream of tartar
½ teaspoon bicarbonate of soda (baking soda)
pinch of salt
50 g (2 oz) butter, chilled and diced
25 g (1 oz) caster (superfine) sugar
125 ml (4 fl oz) milk, plus extra to glaze
butter, honey or jam, to serve

Sift the flour, cream of tartar, bicarbonate of soda (baking soda) and salt into a mixing bowl and rub in the butter with your fingertips until the mixture resembles breadcrumbs. Stir in the sugar and add enough milk to mix to a soft dough.

Turn on to a floured surface, knead lightly and roll out to 2 cm (¾ inch) thick. Cut into 5 cm (2 inch) rounds. Place on a floured baking sheet and brush with milk.

Bake in a preheated oven, 220°C (425°F), Gas Mark 7, for 10 minutes. Transfer to a wire rack to cool. Serve slathered with butter and honey or Bogsberry Preserve (see page 26).

For lavender-flavoured biscuits for Violet, place 125 ml (4 fl oz) milk in a small pan and add 2–3 lavender flowers. Bring to the boil, then immediately remove the pan from the heat and leave to cool. Use the milk to make the biscuits as above.

BOGSBERRY PRESERVE (V)

Thanks to Raeve, we know that a simple chunk of bread topped with a scrape of butter and a dollop of jam can be utterly sublime. This plum, marrow and blackberry homage to that wisdom tastes deliciously sweet-sharp and is surprisingly easy to make. Serve simply with bread, Brennan's honeyed biscuits (see page 24) or a pillow of buttermin loaf.

Makes 6 jars
Preparation time 25 minutes | Cooking time 35–40 minutes

- 1 small marrow (summer squash), 750–875 g (1½–1¾ lb), peeled, halved, deseeded and diced
- 1.5 kg (3 lb) just-ripe plums, quartered and stoned (pitted)
- 250 g (8 oz) blackberries
- 300 ml (½ pint) water
- 1.5 kg (3 lb) granulated sugar, warmed
- 15 g (½ oz) butter (optional)

Add the marrow, plums and blackberries to a preserving pan with the measurement water, then cover and cook for 20 minutes, until the fruit is just tender.

Pour the sugar into the pan and heat gently, stirring from time to time, until dissolved. Bring to the boil, then boil rapidly until setting point is reached (15–20 minutes).

Use a sugar thermometer for a failsafe method, making sure to stir the jam before testing the temperature. For a good set, you need 105°C (221°F). Alternatively, use a flake test: gently stir, then lift the spoon out of the pan and hold so that it is vertical. If the jam forms a large blob or flake that very slowly drops from the spoon, it is ready. If it runs off in a thin stream, it isn't ready, so heat again and retry after a few minutes.

When setting point is reached, skim with a draining spoon or stir in butter if needed.

Ladle into warm, dry jars, filling to the very top. Cover with screw-top lids, or with waxed discs and cellophane tops secured with elastic bands. Label and leave to cool.

GWENDOLINE'S GRAVLAX & CREAM CHEESE BAGELS (V)

Zodiac Academy's Gwendoline likes her bagels buttery, but chewy bagel, rich gravlax and creamy, herby cheese is a magical combination. These quintessential brunchtime bites will fill you up and they're a little bit fancy too.

Serves 2

Preparation time 14 minutes | Cooking time 4–6 minutes

2 poppy and sesame seed bagels, cut in half horizontally
125 g (4 oz) cream cheese
175 g (6 oz) gravlax, finely sliced
2 tablespoons chopped chives
black pepper, plus extra to serve

Put the bagels, cut side down, on a sandwich grill (broiler). Without closing the lid, leave them to toast for 2–3 minutes until golden. Remove from the grill.

Spread the bases with the cream cheese and then top with the gravlax. Scatter the chopped chives over the bagel and season with black pepper.

Top with the bagel lids and return to the sandwich grill. Lower the top plate and toast for 2–3 minutes until golden and crispy. Serve immediately with a sprinkling of black pepper.

DRAGONRIDER CHILLIED BEEF PARCELS

These hot and hearty mini pies pack tender minced beef, spicy tomatoes and creamy, earthy beans into a golden polenta pastry with a powerful crunch – the ultimate protein brunch for on the road or in the air. Eat on their own, or with creamy coleslaw for a hint of sweetness.

Makes 6

Preparation time 30 minutes | Cooking time 1 hour 10 minutes

- 2 teaspoons sunflower oil
- 250 g (8 oz) minced (ground) beef
- 1 small onion, chopped
- 1 garlic clove, finely chopped
- ½ teaspoon dried crushed chillies (chilis)
- ¼ teaspoon ground cinnamon
- 2 teaspoons light muscovado (brown) sugar
- 1 bay leaf
- 200 g (7 oz) can chopped tomatoes
- 200 g (7 oz) can red kidney beans, drained
- 150 ml (¼ pint) beef stock
- beaten egg, to glaze
- salt and black pepper

FOR THE POLENTA PASTRY

- 300 g (10 oz) plain (all-purpose) flour
- 50 g (2 oz) polenta
- 75 g (3 oz) butter, diced
- 75 g (3 oz) white vegetable fat, diced
- 4–4½ tablespoons cold water

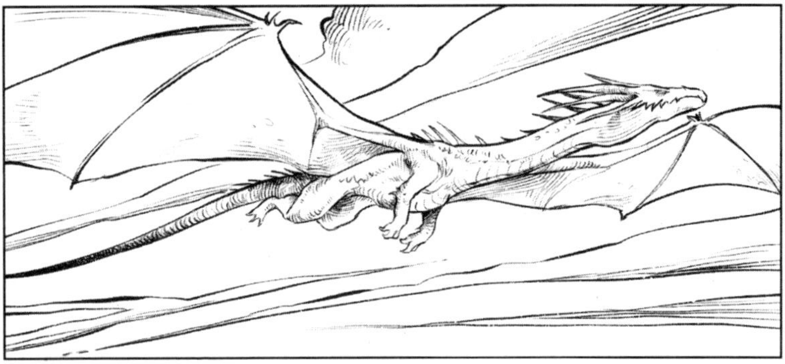

Heat the oil in a saucepan, add the mince (ground beef) and onion and fry, stirring, until the mince is browned. Stir in the garlic, chilies (chilis), cinnamon, sugar and bay leaf. Mix in the tomatoes, kidney beans and stock, then add plenty of salt and pepper. Bring to the boil, stirring, then cover and simmer gently for 45 minutes. Leave to cool.

Make the pastry. Add the flour, polenta, fats and a little salt and pepper to a bowl. Rub in the fats with your fingertips or an electric mixer until you have fine crumbs. Add enough water to form a smooth dough, then knead lightly on a surface dusted with flour. Cut the pastry in half, roll out one half and trim to a 12 × 38 cm (5 ×15 inch) rectangle, then cut into 3 ×12 cm (5 inch) squares.

Spoon half the filling into the centre of the pastry squares. Brush the edges with beaten egg, then bring the points of the pastry up to the centre, pressing the straight edges of the pastry together.

Transfer to an oiled baking sheet and repeat with the remaining pastry and filling to make 6 pies. Brush the pies with beaten egg, then bake in a preheated oven, 190°C (375°F), Gas Mark 5, for 20 minutes. Serve hot straight from the oven or cold straight from your backpack.

HARVEST HAND PIES FOR HEDGE WITCHES (V)

For mid-morning fuel without the meat, these wholesome chilli and pumpkin pies are packed with seasonal energy and have a welcome warming kick – just what you need after a sunrise circle casting or by an autumn campfire. Eat on their own, or with peppery rocket (arugula) salad and sour-cream dressing.

Makes 4

Preparation time 30 minutes | Cooking time 40–45 minutes

1 tablespoon olive oil
1 large red onion, chopped
400 g (13 oz) deseeded pumpkin (or butternut squash if out of season), peeled, cut into small dice
2 cloves garlic, finely chopped
½ teaspoon smoked paprika
400 g (13 oz) can chopped tomatoes
470 g (15 oz) ready-made shortcrust pastry (pie crust), defrosted if frozen
flour, for dusting
100 g (3½ oz) feta cheese, drained, crumbled
beaten egg, to glaze
salt and black pepper

Heat the oil in a saucepan, add the onion and pumpkin and fry for 5 minutes until softened. Stir in the garlic and paprika, then the tomatoes and a little salt and pepper. Cover and simmer for 15 minutes, stirring from time to time until the pumpkin is just cooked.

Cut the pastry (pie crust) into 4 pieces then roll each piece out on a lightly floured surface until large enough to line a buttered 12 cm (5 inch) fluted loose-bottomed tart tin (tart pan). Press over the base and sides, then trim the top level with the tin. Reserve the pastry trimmings.

Put the pies on a baking sheet, spoon in the pumpkin filling, then sprinkle with crumbled feta. Brush the top edge of the pastry with a little beaten egg. Roll out the pastry trimmings and cut into narrow strips, long enough to go over the tops of the pies. Arrange as a lattice on each pie, then brush with a little egg.

Bake in a preheated oven, 180°C (350°F), Gas Mark 4, for 20–25 minutes until golden brown. Leave to stand for 5 minutes, then remove from the tins and serve warm or cold.

VINCENT'S DAWNRISE HOT SHOT (V)

For a power-enhancing start to your day (or night) inspired by *Crowns of Nyaxia*, try this spicy red onion and beetroot juice packed with nutrients and antioxidants to improve blood flow, focus and stamina. It's enough to make a Hiaj king's wings curl.

Makes 200 ml (7 fl oz)
Preparation time 5 minutes

125 g (4 oz) watercress
125 g (4 oz) red onion
1 garlic clove
250 g (8 oz) carrot
125 g (4 oz) beetroot (beets), plus leaves to serve (optional)

Juice the watercress, onion and garlic with the carrot and beetroot (beets). Pour the juice into a glass, decorate with beetroot leaves, if liked, and serve immediately.

Alternatively, for carrot and beetroot juice, peel and roughly chop 2.5 cm (1 inch) cube fresh root ginger and juice the ginger with 10 large carrots and 4 large beetroots. Serve over ice.

WARRIOR LASSI (V)

Our favourite strong frontwomen from Jude Duarte to Caleana Sardothien have shown us that warriors need their strength! This gently spiced cucumber lassi is bursting with nutrients and probiotics for a natural energy boost and midmorning refresher that all warrior women can enjoy.

Makes 400 ml (14 fl oz)
Preparation time 5 minutes

150 g (5 oz) cucumber
150 g (5 oz) live natural (plain) yogurt
100 ml (3½ fl oz) ice-cold still water
handful of mint
½ teaspoon ground cumin
squeeze of lemon

Peel and roughly chop the cucumber. Place in a food processor or blender and add the yogurt and iced water.

Pull the mint leaves off their stalks, reserving a few for decoration. Chop the remainder roughly and put them into the food processor. Add the cumin and lemon juice and process briefly.

Pour the smoothie into a tall glass, decorate with mint leaves, if liked, and serve immediately.

M2M

SPICY SOUPS & ENCHANTING STARTERS

From breaking bread in shadowy taverns to post-battle recovery meals and courtly banquets, eating together is often about community and connection. True, it can also get you cursed or poisoned, but few things say 'I love and trust you' better than a cosy plate of food made especially for two.

There's perhaps no purer expression of food as belonging than a hearty bowl of soup that's been cooked with love and tenderness – it's surely no accident that soup was Feyre's bonding meal of choice.

But that's not the only way to get things started. If you're planning a feast, don't be afraid to put sharing at the heart of the table. Lean into the aesthetic of big, beautiful sharing plates by creating a spread of starters and letting everyone help themselves. (Just think: all those accidentally touching fingertips.)

In this section, you'll find warming, restorative broths to lift your heart and fill your stomach, as well as small homey dishes, lighter plates for courtly splendour and some intimate aphrodisiac tasters – all of them designed to whet the appetite and set the stage.

FEYRE'S GOOD SOUP

This cosy slow-cooked beef and barley soup is full of rustic flavour for serious bonding vibes – a perfect bowl of belonging. Serve piping hot (not boiling) with hunks of crusty bread and butter.

Serves 6

Preparation time 20 minutes | Cooking time 2 hours

- 25 g (1 oz) butter
- 250 g (8 oz) braising beef (chuck steak), fat trimmed away and meat cut into small cubes
- 1 large onion, finely chopped
- 200 g (7 oz) swede (rutabaga), diced
- 150 g (5 oz) carrot, diced
- 100 g (3½ oz) pearl barley
- 2 litres (3½ pints) beef stock
- 2 teaspoons dry English mustard (optional)
- salt and black pepper
- chopped parsley, to garnish

Heat the butter in a large saucepan, add the beef and onion and fry for 5 minutes, stirring, until the beef is browned and the onion just beginning to colour.

Stir in the diced vegetables, pearl barley, stock and mustard, if using. Season with salt and pepper and bring to the boil. Cover and simmer for 1¾ hours, stirring occasionally until the meat and vegetables are very tender. Taste and adjust the seasoning if needed. Ladle the soup into bowls and sprinkle with a little chopped parsley.

CADET RECOVERY BOWL

This protein-rich soup combines smoky chorizo and sweet, creamy broad beans for a hearty bowl with a fiery punch – just what you need when you've pushed yourself to the limit, whether on the Basgiath gauntlet or at the gym. Top with briny green olive tapenade toasts for a restorative autumn supper.

Serves 6

Preparation time 20 minutes | Cooking time 20 minutes

2 tablespoons olive oil
1 large onion, roughly chopped
500 g (1 lb) potatoes, diced
150 g (5 oz) chorizo, diced
4 tomatoes, diced
300 g (10 oz) frozen broad (fava) beans
1.5 litres (2½ pints) chicken stock
salt and black pepper
basil leaves, to garnish

FOR THE OLIVE TAPENADE TOASTS

250 g (8oz) stoned (pitted) green olives
small bunch of fresh basil
4 garlic cloves
2 teaspoons capers, drained
4 tablespoons olive oil
1 tablespoon white wine vinegar
12 slices of French bread

Heat the oil in a large saucepan, add the onion, potatoes and chorizo and fry for 5 minutes, stirring regularly until just beginning to soften.

Stir in the tomatoes, broad (fava) beans and stock, season and bring to the boil. Cover and simmer for 15 minutes until the vegetables are tender.

Mash some of the potatoes roughly with a fork to thicken the soup slightly. Taste and adjust the seasoning if needed.

Meanwhile, make the olive tapendade toasts. Finely chop in a food processor with the basil, 2 of the garlic cloves, the capers, olive oil and white wine vinegar.

Toast the bread on both sides. Halve the remaining 2 garlic cloves then rub one side of the toast with the halves of garlic and spread with the tapenade. Ladle the soup into bowls and top with the tapenade toasts and sprinkle with basil leaves to garnish.

Any remaining tapenade can be stored for up to 2 weeks in the refrigerator in a small jar with the surface covered with a little extra olive oil. It is delicious served with crudités or tossed with pasta.

THE HIDDEN ONES' MIDWINTER BROTH (V)

Like the unseen magic of dark winter forests, this cosy, aromatic kale and chilli broth is full of earthy goodness and unexpected warmth. Topped with chunky garlic and chilli croûtons, it's perfect on its own for a simple kitchen supper – or serve smaller portions to start a courtly feast.

Serves 8–10

Preparation time 20 minutes | Cooking time 50 minutes

50 g (2 oz) butter
1 onion, chopped
2 carrots, sliced
500 g (1 lb) kale, thick stems removed and discarded
1 teaspoon smoked paprika
2 garlic cloves, chopped
1.2 litres (2 pints) water
600 ml (1 pint) vegetable stock
1 tablespoon lemon juice
300 g (10 oz) potatoes, peeled and sliced
pinch of grated nutmeg
salt and black pepper
2 kale leaves, thinly shredded, to garnish

FOR THE GARLIC CROÛTONS

6–8 slices of white or brown bread, crusts removed
6–8 tablespoons olive oil
3 garlic cloves, sliced
¼ teaspoon dried crushed red chilli (red pepper flakes)

Melt the butter or margarine in a large saucepan, add the onion and fry for 5 minutes until softened and just beginning to turn golden. Add the carrots and kale in batches, stirring all the time, and cook for 2 minutes. Add the paprika and garlic and cook for 2 minutes.

Add the measurement water, stock, lemon juice, potatoes and nutmeg, with salt and pepper to taste. Bring to the boil, stirring from time to time. Lower the heat, cover and simmer for 35 minutes or until all the vegetables are soft. Purée the mixture in batches in a blender or food processor, adding extra water if it is too thick.

Prepare the croûtons by cutting the bread into 1 cm (½ inch) cubes. Heat the oil in a large frying pan (skillet), add the garlic and crushed chilli (red pepper flakes) and cook over a moderate heat for 1 minute. Add the bread squares and fry, turning frequently, until evenly golden brown. Transfer the croûtons to kitchen paper (paper towel) with a slotted spoon to drain. Discard the garlic, then add the thinly shredded kale to the pan and fry, stirring constantly until crispy.

Taste the soup and adjust the seasoning if needed and reheat without boiling. Serve in bowls with the garlic croûtons and crispy kale.

QUEEN ISBETH'S CHILLED BLOOD SOUP (V)

As timeless and dark as the Blood Queen herself, this chilled soup brings together a hint of *Blood and Ash* with crunchy celery, deep savoury flavours and a dash of vodka for spicy afterglow. Serve with Gruyère toasted sandwiches for lunch after a late night, or on its own as a showstopping starter.

Serves 6

Preparation time 20 minutes, plus chilling | Cooking time 25 minutes

1 tablespoon olive oil, plus extra to serve
1 onion, chopped
1 red pepper (bell pepper), cored, deseeded and diced
2 celery sticks, sliced
500 g (1 lb) plum tomatoes, chopped
900 ml (1½ pints) vegetable stock
2 teaspoons caster (superfine) sugar
4 teaspoons Worcestershire sauce
4 teaspoons tomato purée (tomato paste)
4 tablespoons vodka
few drops of Tabasco sauce
salt and black pepper
baby celery sticks with leaves, to garnish

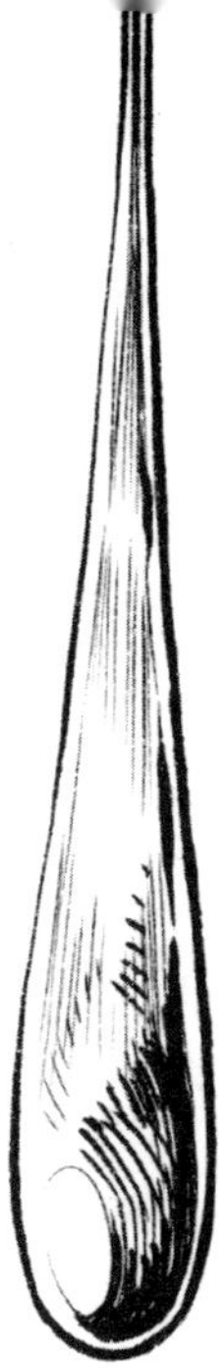

Heat the oil in a saucepan, add the onion and fry for 5 minutes until softened but not browned.

Stir in the red pepper (bell pepper), celery and tomatoes and fry for 5 minutes, stirring occasionally.

Pour in the stock, add the sugar, Worcestershire sauce, tomato purée (tomato paste) and a little salt and pepper and bring to the boil. Cover and simmer for 15 minutes.

Allow the soup to cool slightly, then purée in batches in a blender or food processor until smooth. Sieve if liked then pour back into the saucepan. Add the vodka and Tabasco to taste, and adjust the seasoning if needed. Chill well.

Ladle the soup into small bowls or glasses, add tiny celery sticks, drizzle with a little extra olive oil and sprinkle with a little extra pepper.

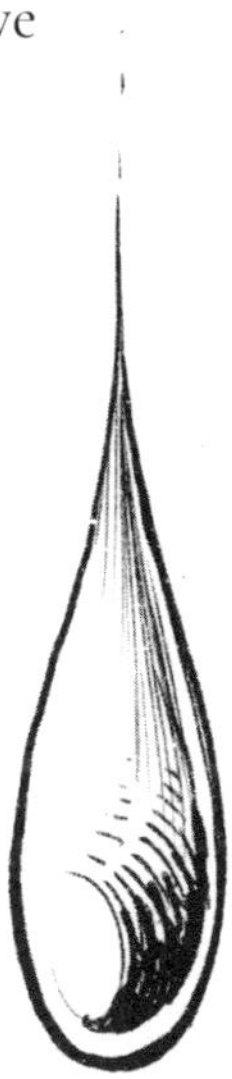

RICH & SPICY HARISSA (V)

If mortal fare is too bland, try adding the flavours of Velaris to spice it up with this warming harissa paste, delicious served with crudités or toasted flatbreads, or to add heat to meals that fill both your stomach and the lingering hole in your chest.

Serves 4 (a little goes a long way)
Preparation time 5 minutes | Cooking time 25 minutes

12 large fresh red chillies (chilis), such as Guajillo, Mexican Horn or New Mexico
3 tablespoons olive oil
1 teaspoon cumin seed
1 teaspoon coriander seeds
1 teaspoon caraway or fennel seeds
3–4 garlic cloves, chopped
1 teaspoon sea salt
1 tablespoon finely chopped fresh coriander (cilantro)
crudités or toasted flatbreads, to serve

Place the chillies (chilis) in an ovenproof dish, pour over the oil and roast in a preheated oven, 200°C (400°F), Gas Mark 6, for 20–25 minutes until the skins begin to buckle. Meanwhile, dry-fry all the seeds in a small, heavy-based frying pan (skillet) over a medium heat for 2–3 minutes until they emit a nutty aroma, then grind in a spice grinder.

Using a small, sharp knife, remove the stalks and skins from the roasted chillies. Slit lengthways and scrape out the seeds. Using a pestle and mortar, pound the chilli flesh, garlic and salt to a smooth paste. Add the spices, mix with 2–3 tablespoons of the roasting oil and stir in the coriander (cilantro).

Spoon the harissa into a small bowl, drizzle over a little more roasting oil and serve with crudités or toasted flatbread. Alternatively, put into a sterilized jar, top with a thin layer of olive oil and seal. (The harissa paste can also be stored in the refrigerator for up to 4 weeks.)

HEAVENLY FIG SALAD

As gifts from the goddesses go, the humble fig is pretty special – a juicy-sweet symbol of fertility and a natural aphrodisiac. This simple salad is a divine celebration of sticky red fig flesh, nutty Serrano ham and peppery rocket that makes a gorgeous summer starter.

Serves 4
Preparation time 10 minutes

- 100 g (3½ oz) rocket (arugula) leaves
- 4 figs, halved or quartered if large
- 150 g (5 oz) Serrano ham, sliced

FOR THE DRESSING

- 1 tablespoon finely chopped shallot
- 1 thyme sprig, leaves stripped and finely chopped
- 1 tablespoon sherry vinegar
- 3 tablespoons extra virgin olive oil
- salt and black pepper

Make the dressing. Mix together the shallot, thyme and vinegar in a bowl. Season well, then whisk in the oil until well combined.

Toss the rocket (arugula) with a little of the dressing, then arrange on a serving plate with the figs and ham. Drizzle over the remaining dressing and serve.

ENEMIES-TO-LOVERS SEARED SCALLOPS WITH MIGAS

Sometimes it's the tension between different flavours and textures that makes a dish sparkle – and no more so than in this little aphrodisiac taster. It's sweet but nutty, simple yet luxurious, with a light, buttery-soft centre inside a crispy, golden, salty migas crust: deliciously confusing. Serve with creamy puréed peas for added sensory goodness.

Serves 4

Preparation time 10 minutes, plus soaking | Cooking time 15 minutes

200 g (7 oz) country-style bread, cut into small cubes
100 ml (3½ fl oz) warm water
pinch of sweet paprika
5 tablespoons olive oil
4 bacon rashers (back bacon)
3 garlic cloves
12 shelled and cleaned plump scallops
salt
chopped parsley, to garnish
lemon slices, to serve

To make the migas, place the bread in a bowl. Mix the measurement water with a little salt and the paprika, then pour over the bread and leave to soak for 30 minutes.

Heat 4 tablespoons of the oil in a large frying pan (skillet), add the bacon and garlic and cook until the bacon is crisp. Remove from the pan, discard the garlic and break the bacon into small pieces.

Squeeze any excess water from the bread, then cook in the pan for 10 minutes, stirring frequently, until crisp and golden. Return the bacon pieces and heat through.

Meanwhile, in a separate frying pan, heat the remaining oil. Pat the scallops dry with kitchen paper (paper towel), season with salt and then fry for 2–3 minutes on each side until golden and just cooked through. Serve sprinkled with the migas and parsley, along with lemon slices.

DOWNWORLDER TUNA CARPACCIO

This dish of paper-thin slices of melt-in-the-mouth fresh tuna is the ultimate feast for werewolves, vampires or mundanes with a taste for raw flesh – even better, it's restaurant-looking food you can make easily at home. Serve on its own or with crusty bread, adding a scattering of nasturtium flowers for a special courtly starter.

Serves 4
Preparation time 10 minutes, plus freezing

250 g (8 oz) piece of tuna loin
juice of 3 lemons
150 ml (¼ pint) extra virgin olive oil
1 garlic clove, finely chopped
1 tablespoon salted capers, rinsed
125 g (4 oz) rocket (arugula) leaves
salt and black pepper
fresh Parmesan cheese shavings, to serve

Trim the tuna of any membrane or gristle. Wrap tightly in clingfilm (plastic wrap) and put in the freezer for about 1 hour until just frozen but not rock solid.

Meanwhile, whisk together the lemon juice, oil, garlic and capers in a bowl. Add salt and pepper to taste and whisk until emulsified.

Unwrap the tuna and thinly slice with a sharp, thin bladed knife. Arrange the slices on 4 large serving plates. Spoon the dressing over the tuna. Top with a tangle of rocket (arugula) leaves and scatter with Parmesan shavings.

NONNA MARIA'S MAGIC CAPONATA (V)

Inspired by Palermo's favourite matriarch, *streghe* coven leader and spellbinding chef, this version of the iconic Sicilian caponata combines soft, sticky aubergines with sweet, sour and savoury flavours that will have you drooling. Serve warm or cold with crusty bread as a rustic starter, or warm with creamy mashed potatoes for a kitchen supper.

Serves 4
Preparation time 15 minutes, plus standing
Cooking time 30 minutes

- 100 ml (3½ fl oz) olive oil
- 2 aubergines (eggplants), cut into 3.5 cm (1½ inch) cubes
- 1 large onion, coarsely chopped
- 3 celery sticks, sliced
- 50 g (2 oz) pine nuts
- 2 garlic cloves, chopped
- 400 g (13 oz) can plum tomatoes, drained and roughly chopped
- 2 tablespoons capers, drained
- 50 g (2 oz) pitted green olives
- 3 tablespoons red wine vinegar
- 1 tablespoon caster (superfine) sugar
- 6 basil leaves
- salt and black pepper

Heat the oil in a large frying pan (skillet) over a high heat until the oil begins to shimmer. Add the aubergine (eggplant), in batches, and cook, stirring frequently, for 5–6 minutes until they are golden and tender. Use a slotted spoon to transfer to a bowl.

Pour away all but 2 tablespoons oil from the pan. Add the onion, celery and pine nuts and cook over a low heat for 10 minutes until the vegetables are softened and lightly golden. Return the aubergines to the pan and stir in the remaining ingredients, except for the basil. Season with salt and pepper.

Bring the pan to the boil, then reduce the heat and simmer for 5 minutes. Stir in the basil. Remove from the heat and leave to stand for at least 15 minutes to allow the flavours to mingle.

Serve warm or cold, as an antipasto, side dish or as a vegetarian main course, with some bread on the side.

SPRING COURT RICOTTA & PEA CROSTINI

This dish of crunchy toasted bread topped with a fragrant, creamy ricotta and pea pesto could be freshly plucked from the Spring Court's green hills and forests – a divine springtime bite for humans and High Fae alike. Serve sprinkled with walnuts and grated lemon zest for extra pizazz.

Serves 6

Preparation time 10 minutes, plus cooling | Cooking time 10 minutes

1 small French stick, sliced
3 tablespoons extra virgin olive oil, plus extra to serve
250 g (8 oz) fresh or frozen shelled peas
1 small garlic clove, crushed
50 g (2 oz) ricotta cheese
juice of ½ lemon
1 tablespoon chopped mint
15 g (½ oz) Parmesan cheese, freshly grated
salt and black pepper

Lay the bread slices on a baking sheet, brush lightly with 1 tablespoon of the oil and bake in a preheated oven, 190°C (375°F), Gas Mark 5, for 5–6 minutes until crisp and golden. Leave to cool on a wire rack while you prepare the pesto.

Cook the peas in a saucepan of lightly salted boiling water for 3 minutes. Drain and immediately refresh under cold water. Put the peas in a food processor, add the remaining oil, the garlic, ricotta, lemon juice, mint, Parmesan and salt and pepper and process until fairly smooth.

Spread the crostini with the pesto and serve drizzled with oil.

HIGH-STAKES BLUE CHEESE SOUFFLÉS (V)

From Phantasma to the Purging Trials, there's nothing quite like a high-stakes challenge – and while cooking soufflés isn't *quite* so dramatic, they do have a bit of a nerve-wracking reputation. Fear not: these deliciously rich and airy blue cheese soufflés look impressive but are secretly easy to make.

Serves 6

Preparation time 15 minutes, plus soaking | Cooking time 10-15 minutes

75 g (3 oz) crustless sourdough bread, cut into chunks
250 ml (8 fl oz) milk
150 g (5 oz) blue cheese, crumbled
50 g (2 oz) butter, softened, plus extra for greasing
4 eggs, separated
1 tablespoon white wine vinegar
3 tablespoons olive oil
1 teaspoon walnut oil
1 red apple, cored and thinly sliced
handful of rocket leaves
salt and black pepper

Put the bread in a bowl and pour over the milk. Leave to soak for 5 minutes, then squeeze any excess milk from the bread.

Transfer the bread to a food processor or blender with the cheese, butter and egg yolks and blend until smooth. Season to taste.

Whisk the egg whites in a large, grease-free bowl until stiff peaks form. Stir a large spoonful into the cheese mixture, then carefully fold in the remainder, half at a time. Spoon the mixture into 6 x 150 ml (¼ pint) well-greased ramekins and bake in a preheated oven, 220°C (425°F), Gas Mark 7, for 10–15 minutes until puffed and golden.

Meanwhile, whisk together the vinegar, olive oil and walnut oil and season to taste. Toss together with the apple and rocket leaves. Serve the soufflés immediately with the dressed rocket and apple alongside.

PERSEPHONE'S POMEGRANATE PROMISE (V)

Pomegranate seeds are unlikely to land you in an eternal cycle of death and rebirth, but they've long been tied to love and fertility and are considered a natural aphrodisiac. In a fiery salsa served with sharp, salty haloumi, these tiny pink jewels make a spicy addition to any table.

Serves 4

Preparation time 10 minutes | Cooking time 5 minutes

500 g (1 lb) haloumi cheese, sliced
1 tablespoon clear honey

FOR THE POMEGRANATE SALSA

½ pomegranate
4 tablespoons extra virgin olive oil
2 tablespoons chopped parsley
1 tablespoon lemon juice
1 small red chilli (chili), deseeded and finely chopped
1 small garlic clove, crushed
1 teaspoon pomegranate syrup (optional)
salt and black pepper

First make the pomegranate salsa. Carefully scoop the pomegranate seeds into a bowl, discarding all the white membrane. Stir in the remaining ingredients and season with salt and pepper.

Heat a large nonstick frying pan for 2–3 minutes until hot. Add the haloumi slices, in batches, and cook over a high heat for about 60 seconds on each side until browned and softened. Meanwhile, warm the honey in a small saucepan until runny.

Transfer the pan-fried haloumi to serving plates and spoon over the salsa. Drizzle the honey over the haloumi and salsa, and serve immediately.

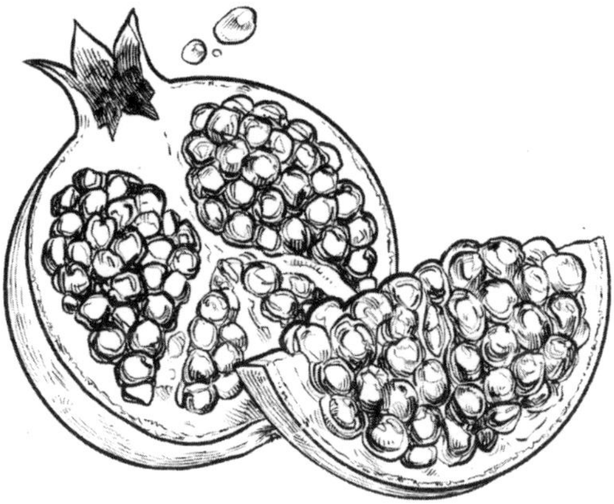

ELVEN PADRÓN ROULETTE (V)

Hidden identity is essential to the job for heroines like Romy Watts, but you don't have to wake up in the body of an elven princess to enjoy a spicy guessing game. The unpredictable heat factor of Padrón peppers gives this delicious tapas staple a hot twist – you just won't know *how* hot till you try them.

Serves 6

Preparation time 5 minutes | Cooking time 3–5 minutes

3 tablespoons olive oil
250 g (8 oz) Padrón peppers or baby green (bell) peppers, or mild green chillies (chilis)
sea salt flakes

Heat the oil in a large frying pan (skillet), add the peppers or chillies and cook over a high heat for 3–5 minutes, turning frequently, until the skins start to brown. Remove from the pan and drain on kitchen paper (paper towel), then serve scattered with sea salt flakes.

MAIN PLATES FOR ENEMIES & LOVERS

Assuming nobody has started a war, discovered their hitherto secret vampirine lineage or received an unexpected visit from the devil himself, your guests should by now be settled in and ready for the main event.

In realms all the way from Dhomm to Prythian, feasts are high-society, high-tension events with as much political intrigue and illicit romance as religious ritual and tradition. Let's face it: for every strengthened alliance or observed ancient pact there's someone giving the forbidden fruit a lingering look, and that's at bare minimum.

Us mortals might not spend three days wearing evergreen garlands and gifting each other riverside estates under a cursed candelabra, but we can enjoy sitting down with people we care about to eat some fabulous food. It doesn't have to be about abundance, either – sharing a simple, comforting stew can go a long way to mending a battle-weary heart and is sometimes all we need.

So, in this section you'll find spicy stews, hearty meats and vibrant seasonal vegetable dishes to delight whether you're cooking a cosy Tuesday supper or a lavish feast for friends and lovers.

EMPYREAN JUNIPER ROAST LAMB

What better feast for dragons and humans than succulent roast lamb? Here, white wine and piney juniper aromatics balance the meat's richness and lend mysterious majesty to this perennial favourite. Serve with minted peas, crispy roast potatoes and a gravy made from the meat juices.

Serves 6

Preparation time 20 minutes | Cooking time 1 hour 35 minutes

- 2 tablespoons olive oil
- 1 leg of lamb, about 1.5 kg (3 lb), trimmed of excess fat
- 10 juniper berries, crushed
- 3 garlic cloves, crushed
- 50 g (2 oz) salted anchovies, boned and rinsed
- 1 tablespoon chopped rosemary
- 2 tablespoons balsamic vinegar
- 2 rosemary sprigs
- 300 ml (½ pint) dry white wine
- salt and black pepper

Heat the oil over a medium heat in a roasting tin in which the lamb will fit snugly. Add the lamb and cook until browned all over. Leave to cool.

Pound 6 of the juniper berries, the garlic, anchovies and chopped rosemary with the end of a rolling pin in a bowl. Stir in the vinegar and mix to a paste.

Make small incisions all over the lamb with a small, sharp knife. Spread the paste over the lamb, working it into the incisions. Season with salt and pepper. Put the rosemary sprigs in the roasting tin and put the lamb on top. Pour in the wine and add the remaining juniper berries.

Cover the roasting tin with foil and bring to the boil, then cook in a preheated oven, 160°C (325°F), Gas Mark 3, for 1 hour, turning the lamb every 20 minutes. Raise the temperature to 200°C (400°F), Gas Mark 6, uncover and roast for a further 30 minutes until the lamb is very tender.

BEYOND THE WALL GAME PIE

You don't need to be a huntress like Feyre to snare this succulent game pie. Packed with juicy pheasant and pigeon, topped with golden puff pastry, it's a wild taste of the woods and perfect for a rustic winter's feast – in cottage or castle. Serve with robust seasonal veg, such as sprouts and red cabbage.

Serves 4

Preparation time 45 minutes | Cooking time 2 hours

25 g (1 oz) butter
1 tablespoon olive oil
1 oven-ready pheasant, halved
1 oven-ready pigeon, halved
2 rabbit or chicken leg joints
1 large onion, roughly chopped
100 g (3½ oz) smoked streaky bacon, diced
2 tablespoons plain (all-purpose) flour
200 ml (7 fl oz) red wine
400 ml (13 fl oz) chicken stock
2 tablespoons redcurrant jelly
1 teaspoon juniper or allspice berries, roughly crushed
1 bouquet garni
flour, for dusting
375 g (12 oz) ready-made puff pastry, defrosted if frozen
beaten egg, to glaze
salt and black pepper

Heat the butter and oil in a large frying pan (skillet), then fry the game, in batches, until browned. Lift out and put into a large casserole dish. Add the onion and bacon to the frying pan and fry for 5 minutes, stirring until golden.

Mix in the flour, then stir in the wine, stock and redcurrant jelly. Add the berries, bouquet garni and seasoning, then bring to the boil. Tip the sauce over the game, cover and cook in a preheated oven, 160°C (325°F), Gas Mark 3, for 1¼ hours.

Leave to cool. Lift out the game and take the meat off the bone. Return the meat to the sauce, discard the bouquet garni, then spoon into a 1.2 litre (2 pint) pie dish.

Roll out the pastry on a lightly floured surface until a little larger than the top of the pie dish. Cut 1 cm (½ inch) wide strips from the edges and stick on to the dish rim with beaten egg. Brush the pastry strips with egg and lay the sheet of pastry on top. Press down, trim off the excess then flute the edges. Cut leaves from the rerolled trimmings and decorate.

Brush the pie with beaten egg, then cook in a preheated oven, 200°C (400°F), Gas Mark 6, for 30–35 minutes until golden and piping hot inside.

KEJARI VICTORY GOULASH

Not all victories involve wildcards and bloodspill, but they all deserve celebration. This rich and soothing blood-red stew brings together sweet, earthy beetroot, slow-cooked spices and meat so tender it falls apart – a delicious dish for sharing to mark successes big and small. Serve with creamy swede and carrot mash and a bitter-leaf salad.

Serves 4

Preparation time 30 minutes | Cooking time 2½ hours

- 2 tablespoons olive oil
- 450 g (14½ oz) lean pork, diced
- 2 onions, sliced
- 1 teaspoon hot smoked paprika
- 1 teaspoon caraway seeds
- 750 g (1½ lb) piece of smoked bacon knuckle
- 3 bay leaves
- 1.2 litres (2 pints) water
- 300 g (10 oz) beetroot (beets), peeled and diced
- 300 g (10 oz) red cabbage, finely sliced
- 3 tablespoons tomato purée (tomato paste)

FOR THE SWEDE AND CARROT MASH

- 500 g (1 lb) carrots
- 1 kg (2 lb) swede (rutabaga), peeled and cut into chunks
- 1 teaspoon fresh thyme (chopped)
- 3 tablespoons olive oil

Heat the oil in a large saucepan and fry the diced pork until browned. Add the onions, paprika and caraway and fry gently for a further 5 minutes until the onions are browned.

Add the piece of bacon knuckle, the bay leaves and measurement water. Bring to the boil, cover with a lid and reduce the heat to the lowest setting. Cook very gently for about 2 hours until the bacon knuckle is very tender and the meat falls easily from the bone.

Remove the knuckle and leave until cool enough to handle. Pull the meat from the bone and shred it back into the pan, discarding the skin and bone.

Add the beetroot (beets), cabbage and tomato purée (tomato paste) to the pan and cook gently, covered, for about 15 minutes until the beetroot and cabbage are tender. Check the seasoning and serve.

For swede and carrot mash to serve as an accompaniment, cook the carrots in boiling water for 10 minutes. Add the swede (rutabaga) and cook until tender. Drain thoroughly and return to the pan. Mash with the thyme and olive oil.

HOT SKEWERED CHICKEN

You can make these smoking-hot chicken kebabs with a cursed sword or regular kitchen skewers – either way, you'll get tender, juicy chicken pieces cooked in a spicy marinade and then slathered in a zesty chilli dip. Serve with warm flatbreads, rice and crispy salad leaves for a truly *Swordheart* supper.

Serves 4

Preparation time 15 minutes, plus marinating | Cooking time 15 minutes

800 g (1¾ lb) skinless chicken thigh fillets, cut into bite-sized pieces
30 g (1 oz) fresh coriander (cilantro), chopped
30 g (1 oz) mint, chopped
1 teaspoon coarse black pepper
juice of 2 lemons
1 teaspoon light muscovado sugar
2 teaspoons peeled and finely grated fresh root ginger
2 garlic cloves, crushed
200 ml (7 fl oz) natural (plain) yogurt
lemon wedges, to serve

FOR THE DIP

125 ml (4 fl oz) rice or wine vinegar
2 tablespoons caster (superfine) sugar
1 red chilli (chili), finely diced
½ red onion, finely diced
6 tablespoons finely diced cucumber

Put the chicken in a shallow non-reactive bowl. Put the herbs, pepper, lemon juice, sugar, ginger, garlic and yogurt in a food processor or blender and blend until smooth. Pour the mixture over the chicken and toss to coat evenly, then cover and leave to marinate for 10–15 minutes.

Meanwhile, make the dip. Heat the vinegar and sugar in a small saucepan until the sugar has dissolved, then increase the heat and boil for 3 minutes until slightly syrupy. Remove from the heat and stir in the red chilli (chili) and red onion. Leave to cool. When cool, stir in the cucumber and set aside.

Thread the chicken on to 12 metal skewers, then cook under a preheated medium-hot grill (broiler) for 4–5 minutes on each side or until cooked through. Transfer the skewers on to 4 serving plates and drizzle over a little of the dip. Serve with the remaining dip and lemon wedges to squeeze over.

SENSITIVELY SPICED ILLYRIAN WINGS

Illyrian wings may be big and powerful, but they're also very sensitive and responsive to a gentle stroke. Pay tribute to your favourite pair of wings with the big flavours and smoky spicing of these grilled harissa chicken wings with sweet burnt orange segments.

Serves 4
Preparation time 10 minutes, plus marinating
Cooking time 8 minutes

1 tablespoon Rich & Spicy harissa (see page 48)
2 tablespoons olive oil
small bunch of coriander (cilantro), finely chopped
8–12 chicken wings
salt
small bunch of flat leaf parsley, roughly chopped, to garnish

FOR THE ORANGES
2 oranges, cut into quarters
2 tablespoons icing (confectioners') sugar

In a bowl, beat the harissa into the oil, season with salt and stir in the coriander (cilantro). Put the chicken wings into a non-reactive dish and brush over the harissa oil. Cover and leave to marinate for 15 minutes.

Cook the marinated wings over a hot barbecue or under a preheated hot grill (broiler), basting with any remaining harissa oil, for 3–4 minutes on each side until cooked through.

Meanwhile, dip the oranges into the icing (confectioners') sugar and cook over the barbecue or under a preheated hot grill for about 2–3 minutes on each side until slightly burned but not black.

Serve the chicken and oranges garnished with the parsley.

BLOOD-LUST DEVILLED FILLET STEAKS

These sizzling steaks cooked in a dark, spicy sauce have a tangy, caramelized exterior and tender, juicy interior – a wickedly delicious unholy union to sink your fangs into. Serve with creamy garlic mash and dark, juicy greens for a majestic main course.

Serves 4

Preparation time 10 minutes | Cooking time 10 minutes

2 tablespoons olive oil
4 fillet steaks, about 175 g (6 oz) each
2 tablespoons balsamic vinegar
75 ml (3 fl oz) full-bodied red wine
4 tablespoons beef stock
2 garlic cloves, chopped
1 teaspoon crushed fennel seeds
1 tablespoon sun-dried tomato purée (tomato paste)
½ teaspoon crushed dried chillies (red pepper flakes)
salt and black pepper
chopped flat leaf parsley (optional)
rocket (arugula) leaves (optional)

Heat the oil in a nonstick frying pan (skillet) until smoking hot. Add the steaks and cook over a very high heat for about 2 minutes on each side, if you want your steaks to be medium rare. Remove to a plate, season with salt and pepper and keep warm in a low oven.

Pour the vinegar, wine and stock into the pan and boil for 30 seconds, scraping any sediment from the base of the pan. Add the garlic and fennel seeds and whisk in the sun-dried tomato purée (tomato paste) and crushed chillies (red pepper flakes).

Bring the sauce to the boil and boil fast to reduce until syrupy. Transfer the steaks to serving plates, pouring any collected meat juices into the sauce. Return the sauce to the boil, then season with salt and pepper.

Pour the sauce over the steaks and serve immediately, garnished with chopped parsley and rocket (arugula) leaves, if liked. Slice the steaks before serving, if you wish.

SEVENDA'S FISH TAGINE

This aromatic dish has flavours of Velaris with flaky, slow-cooked fish infused with fragrant spices in a rich, savoury sauce to fill your tummy and soothe your soul, just like Sevenda's restaurant fare. Serve with buttered saffron rice or sweet potatoes for a truly restorative treat.

Serves 4

Preparation time 15 minutes | Cooking time 55 minutes

750 g (1½ lb) firm white fish fillets, such as cod, sea bass or monkfish, pin-boned, skinned and cut into 5 cm (2 inch) chunks
½ teaspoon cumin seeds
½ teaspoon coriander seeds
6 cardamom pods
4 tablespoons olive oil
2 small onions, thinly sliced
2 garlic cloves, crushed
¼ teaspoon ground turmeric
1 cinnamon stick
40 g (1½ oz) sultanas (golden raisins)
25 g (1 oz) pine nuts, lightly toasted
150 ml (¼ pint) fish stock
finely grated zest of 1 lemon, plus 1 tablespoon juice
salt and black pepper
chopped parsley, to garnish

Season the fish with salt and pepper. Using a pestle and mortar, crush the cumin and coriander seeds and cardamom pods. Discard the cardamom pods, leaving the seeds.

Heat the oil in a large, shallow frying pan (skillet) and fry the onions gently for 6–8 minutes until golden. Add the garlic, crushed spices, turmeric and cinnamon and fry gently, stirring, for 2 minutes. Add the fish pieces, turning them until they are coated in the oil.

Transfer the fish and onions to an ovenproof casserole dish and scatter with the sultanas (golden raisins) and pine nuts. Add the stock and lemon zest and juice to the frying pan and bring the mixture to the boil.

Pour the mixture around the fish, then cover and bake in a preheated oven, 160°C (325°F), Gas Mark 3, for 40 minutes. Garnish with parsley before serving.

SUMMER COURT SALMON EN CROÛTE

Capture the essence of the Summer Court with tender, flaky salmon and fresh green asparagus encased in a buttery pastry shell that's as golden as the beaches – a beautiful seasonal centrepiece to wow High Fae and humans alike. Serve with buttered baby new potatoes and watercress.

Serves 4

Preparation time 25 minutes | Cooking time 40–45 minutes

25 g (1 oz) butter
175 g (6 oz) asparagus, trimmed
600–625 g (1 lb 2 oz–1 lb 4 oz) salmon fillet, about 18–20 cm (7–8 inches) long, skinned
juice of ½ lemon
flour, for dusting
500 g (1 lb) ready-made puff pastry, defrosted if frozen
100 g (3½ oz) medium-fat soft cheese
grated zest of 1 lemon
1 tablespoon chopped tarragon
2 tablespoons chopped parsley
1½ teaspoons green peppercorns, drained and chopped (optional)
50 g (2 oz) sunblush tomatoes, drained and roughly chopped
beaten egg, to glaze
salt flakes, for sprinkling (optional)
salt and black pepper

Heat the butter in a frying pan, add the asparagus and fry for 2–3 minutes until just softened, then season with salt and pepper. Drizzle the salmon with lemon juice and season.

Roll the pastry out thinly on a lightly floured surface and trim to a 35 cm (14 inch) square, then trim a 3.5 cm (1½ inch) strip off one of the sides. Put the salmon on top so that the long side of the salmon is parallel with the narrower side of the pastry rectangle.

Dot the cheese on top of the salmon, then sprinkle with the lemon zest, herbs, peppercorns if using, and tomatoes. Arrange the asparagus on top, alternating their direction.

Brush the pastry around the salmon with beaten egg, then fold the narrower sides up and over the salmon, pressing to seal. Cut the excess from the top ends of pastry, then fold and press to wrap the salmon like a parcel.

Brush the parcel with beaten egg and transfer to a baking sheet. Decorate with cutouts from the pastry trimmings and sprinkle with salt flakes, if using. Bake in a preheated oven, 200°C (400°F), Gas Mark 6, for 35–40 minutes. Check after 25 minutes and cover with foil if the pastry seems to be browning too quickly. To test if the salmon is cooked, insert a knife into the centre, wait 3 seconds, then remove; if the knife feels hot it is cooked.

Cut into thick slices and serve with lemon wedges.

SPELLCASTER SARDE A BECCAFICO

This dish probably *won't* bring about an ancient witch's prophecy, but fresh sardines stuffed with fennel, citrus, breadcrumbs and raisins make a sweet-salty bit of magic for a rustic feast or simple supper. Serve as it is, or with boiled new potatoes and tomato salad.

Serves 4
Preparation time 15 minutes, plus cooling
Cooking time 25 minutes

4 tablespoons extra virgin olive oil
1 fennel bulb, thinly sliced
1 onion, thinly sliced
pared rind of 1 small orange
pared rind of 1 lemon
1 tablespoon roughly chopped dill
1 teaspoon fennel seeds
¼ teaspoon crushed dried chillies (red pepper flakes)
2 garlic cloves, finely chopped
5 tablespoons fresh white breadcrumbs
2 tablespoons roughly chopped flat leaf parsley
4 large or 8 small sardines, filleted
juice of ½ lemon
salt
lemon wedges, to serve

Pour half the oil into a large, heavy-based frying pan (skillet) and stir in the fennel and onion. Add the citrus rind, dill, fennel seeds and crushed chillies (red pepper flakes) and place the pan over a very low heat.

Cook, stirring frequently, for 12–15 minutes until the fennel and onion are golden and caramelized, being careful not to burn. Add the garlic and cook, stirring, for 2 minutes.

Remove from the heat and stir in half the breadcrumbs and parsley. Season with salt and leave to cool.

Drizzle 1 tablespoon of the remaining oil over a large baking sheet. Add half the sardine fillets, skin side down. Season lightly with salt, then spread the fennel mixture over each fillet. Press a second fillet on top, skin side up, and scatter with the remaining breadcrumbs and parsley. Drizzle with the remaining oil and squeeze the lemon juice over the fish. Season again with salt.

Cook under a preheated high grill (broiler) for 6–8 minutes until the fish is opaque all the way through. Serve with lemon wedges.

SIREN'S CALL OYSTER & MUSHROOM BRIOCHE

Indulged in by lovers for thousands of years, oysters evoke the siren call of the ocean which might just pull you under. Serve them with earthy mushrooms, sweet brioche and crispy bacon for the ultimate pairing of land and sea.

Serves 4

Preparation time 10 minutes | Cooking time 15 minutes

- 150 ml (¼ pint) dry white wine or Champagne
- 2 shallots, finely chopped
- 100 ml (3½ fl oz) double (heavy) cream
- 25 g (1 oz) butter
- 2 pancetta rashers (strips), sliced into thin matchsticks
- 75 g (3 oz) oyster mushrooms, halved if large
- 8 oysters, shucked (reserving the liquor)
- 4 individual brioche breads
- handful of chives, finely chopped, plus extra to garnish (optional)

Boil the wine or Champagne with the shallots in a saucepan until reduced by half. Add the cream and cook until you have a rich, creamy sauce.

Heat 15 g (½ oz) of the butter in a frying pan (skillet). Add the pancetta and cook for 2 minutes until turning golden, then add the mushrooms and cook for 3 minutes until browned all over. Add to the sauce with the oysters and their liquor and cook for 2 minutes.

Meanwhile, slice the lid off each brioche and pull out most of the bread inside. Melt the remaining butter in a small saucepan and brush all over the inside of the brioche. Place on a baking sheet in a preheated oven, 200°C (400°F), Gas Mark 6, for 5–10 minutes until crisp.

Stir the chives into the sauce, then spoon into the brioche pots, scatter with more chives, if liked, and serve.

VERY IRREGULAR PUMPKIN RISOTTO

Like a gift from the Nowhere House, this creamy pumpkin and sage risotto packs a punch thanks to the addition of chilli. Eat as it is for a cosy supper by the fire, or serve with a side of peppery rocket (arugula) and lemon salad for an elegant dinner-party main.

Serves 6

Preparation time 20 minutes | Cooking time 40 minutes

100 g (3½ oz) butter
1 large onion, finely chopped
1 fresh or dried red chilli (chili), deseeded and finely chopped
500 g (1 lb) pumpkin, peeled, deseeded and roughly chopped
500 g (1 lb) arborio, carnaroli or vialone nano rice
1.5 litres (2½ pints) chicken or vegetable stock, simmering
3 tablespoons chopped sage, plus extra sprigs to garnish
75 g (3 oz) Parmesan cheese, freshly grated
salt and black pepper

Melt half the butter in a large saucepan over a low heat. Add the onion and cook for 10 minutes until softened. Add the chilli (chili) and cook, stirring, for 1 minute. Add the pumpkin and cook, stirring constantly, for 5 minutes. Add the rice and cook, stirring, for 2 minutes.

Add a large ladleful of the simmering stock. Slowly simmer, stirring constantly, until the stock has been absorbed and the rice parts when a wooden spoon is run through it. Add another ladleful of stock and continue to cook, stirring and adding the stock in ladlefuls, for about 20 minutes until the rice is creamy and almost tender to the bite and the pumpkin is beginning to disintegrate.

Season well with salt and pepper. Remove from the heat and add the chopped sage, remaining butter and the Parmesan. Stir vigorously for 15 seconds. Cover with a tight-fitting lid and leave to stand for a few minutes. Garnish with sage sprigs to serve.

LAIA OF SERRA'S WILD MUSHROOM LASAGNE

Whether you're feeding the Resistance or your *Ember in the Ashes* reading group, the umami bomb of garlic, Parmesan and earthy wild mushrooms that fills each rich, creamy layer of this lasagne is sure to please. Serve with a side of roasted asparagus or bitter chicory (endive) salad to elevate the savoury flavours.

Serves 6

Preparation time 20 minutes, plus cooling | Cooking time 45 minutes

- 100 g (3½ oz) unsalted butter, plus extra for greasing
- 4 tablespoons plain (all-purpose) flour
- 1 litre (1¾ pints) milk
- large pinch of freshly grated nutmeg
- 3 tablespoons roughly chopped flat leaf parsley
- 5 tablespoons freshly grated Parmesan cheese
- 1 tablespoon olive oil
- 625 g (1¼ lb) mixed wild mushrooms, trimmed and thickly sliced
- 1 garlic clove, crushed
- 100 ml (3½ fl oz) dry white wine
- 25 g (1 oz) dried porcini mushrooms, soaked in 100 ml (3½ fl oz) hot water for 10 minutes
- 300 g (10 oz) fresh lasagne sheets
- truffle oil, for drizzling
- salt and black pepper

Melt half the butter in a saucepan over a low heat. Add the flour and cook, stirring with a wooden spoon, for 1–2 minutes until a pale biscuity colour.

Remove from the heat and gradually stir in the milk until smooth. Return to a medium heat and cook, stirring constantly, until thick and velvety.

Add the nutmeg and season with salt and pepper, then stir in the parsley and 2 tablespoons of the Parmesan. Remove from the heat and leave to cool to room temperature.

Melt the remaining butter with the oil in a large, heavy-based frying pan (skillet). Add the fresh mushrooms and cook over a high heat for 2 minutes.

Stir in the garlic and cook for 1 minute. Season with salt and pepper. Pour in the wine and porcini and their soaking water. Cook, stirring, until the liquid has evaporated. Stir into the white sauce.

Grease an ovenproof dish, about 19 x 30 cm (8 x 12 inches). Cover the base with a layer of slightly overlapping lasagne sheets. Top with a quarter of the sauce, then continue layering, finishing with a layer of sauce. Scatter with the remaining Parmesan.

Bake in a preheated oven, 200°C (400°F), Gas Mark 6, for 30 minutes. Drizzle lightly with truffle oil to serve.

FIRE CASSEROLE FOR THE KINGMAKER V

You don't need clairvoyancy skills to know that this nutrient-packed and sticky-soft fennel, Pernod and orange casserole is good for you – the fiery colours and flavours say it all. Serve with hunks of bread or fluffy herby rice for a dazzling courtly main.

Serves 4

Preparation time 15 minutes | Cooking time 50 minutes

- 2 fennel bulbs, trimmed
- 4 tablespoons extra virgin olive oil
- 1 onion, chopped
- 2 garlic cloves, crushed
- 2 teaspoons chopped rosemary
- salt and black pepper
- 100 ml (3½ fl oz) Pernod
- 400 g (13 oz) can chopped tomatoes
- ¼ teaspoon saffron threads
- 2 strips of orange rind
- 2 tablespoons chopped fennel fronds

Cut the fennel lengthways into 5 mm (¼ inch) thick slices. Heat half the oil in a flameproof casserole, add the fennel slices, in batches, and cook over a medium heat for 3–4 minutes on each side until golden. Remove with a slotted spoon.

Heat the remaining oil in the casserole, add the onion, garlic, rosemary and salt and pepper and cook over a low heat, stirring frequently, for 5 minutes. Add the Pernod, bring to the boil and boil until reduced by half. Add the tomatoes, saffron and orange rind and stir well. Arrange the fennel slices over the top.

Bring the casserole to the boil, then cover with a tight-fitting lid and bake in a preheated oven, 180°C (350°F), Gas Mark 4, for 35 minutes until the fennel is tender. Stir in the fennel fronds and serve the casserole hot.

THE WOOD QUEEN'S GOATS' CHEESE & BEETROOT TART V

The vibrant colour and sweet, earthy flavours of this simple rustic tart could come straight from the enchanted forests of ancient Polish folklore. Serve with sides of buttered new potatoes and pickled red onions to contrast with the beetroot's sweetness.

Serves 6
Preparation time 30 minutes, plus chilling
Cooking time 45–50 minutes

- 470 g (15 oz) ready-made shortcrust pastry (pie crust), defrosted if frozen
- 1 tablespoon olive oil
- 1 onion, chopped
- 200 g (7 oz) raw, trimmed beetroot (beets), peeled and coarsely grated
- 4 eggs
- 250 ml (8 fl oz) milk
- 1 teaspoon Dijon mustard
- small bunch of thyme
- 150 g (5 oz) goats' cheese log
- salt and cayenne pepper

Roll the pastry (pie crust) out on a lightly floured surface until a little larger than a buttered 24 cm (9½ inch) fluted loose-bottomed tart tin (tart pan). Lift the pastry over a rolling pin, drape into the tin, then press over the base and sides.

Trim off the excess pastry with scissors so that it stands a little above the top of the tin. Chill for 15 minutes.

Meanwhile, heat the oil in a frying pan (skillet), add the onion and fry until softened. Add the beetroot (beets) and cook for 2–3 minutes. Beat the eggs, milk and mustard together in a bowl. Add the onions, some of the thyme leaves torn from the stems and a generous amount of salt and cayenne pepper. Leave to stand for 5 minutes.

Put the tart case on a baking sheet and pour the beetroot mix into the tart case. Cut the cheese into 6 thick slices, arrange in a ring on top of the tart and sprinkle with the remaining thyme leaves and a little salt and cayenne pepper.

Bake in a preheated oven, 180°C (350°F), Gas Mark 4, for 40–45 minutes until the filling is set. Leave to cool for 15 minutes, then remove the tin and transfer to a plate. Serve warm or cold, cut into wedges.

FAIRY RING PIZZA & ROCKET SALAD

Mortals walking in the woods should beware of stepping into a fairy ring: a circle of mushrooms or toadstools on the ground left by fairies or elves dancing at night – enter at your peril, who knows where it might take you?

Serves 2

Preparation time 10 minutes | Cooking time 8 minutes

1 ready-made thin and crispy pizza base
2 tablespoons onion relish
2 tomatoes, thinly sliced
50 g (2 oz) button mushrooms, thinly sliced
150 g (5 oz) goats' cheese with rind, thinly sliced
2 tablespoons extra virgin olive oil
2 tablespoons ready-made basil pesto
salt and black pepper
rocket (arugula) leaves, to garnish

FOR THE SALAD DRESSING

4 tablespoons lemon juice
2 tablespoons olive oil
½ teaspoon Dijon mustard
salt and black pepper

FOR THE SALAD

250 g (8 oz) rocket
20 g (¾ oz) finely grated Parmesan cheese
40 g (1½ oz) fresh Parmesan cheese shavings

Spread the pizza base with the onion relish. Scatter the tomatoes over the relish. Arrange the mushrooms and slices of goats' cheese in a ring on top. Sprinkle with salt and pepper, drizzle with 1 tablespoon of the oil.

Cook the pizza in a preheated oven 200°C (400°F), Gas Mark 6, for about 8 minutes until the cheese is melting. While cooking, blend the pesto with the remaining olive oil.

Make the salad dressing by whisking the lemon juice, oil and mustard. Season to taste with salt and pepper.

Make the salad. Put the rocket (arugula) leaves in a large salad bowl, sprinkle over the grated Parmesan and mix lightly. Pour over the dressing and toss to combine. Garnish the salad with the Parmesan shavings.

Drizzle the cooked pizza with the pesto mixture and scatter with rocket to garnish. Cut the pizza into slices and serve with the rocket salad.

SWEET TREATS & DESSERTS FOR DESIRE

Sometimes all the high drama and constant sense of imminent danger get a bit much and we need straight-up comfort and indulgence. Chocolate cake with a lemon drizzle chaser might not make everything better, but it helps. Put it this way: if you're looking for a low-stakes love language, you could do a lot worse than a sticky cinnamon bun slathered with too much sugary frosting.

Of course, sweet things can play a more…interesting role too (here's looking at you, Casteel). But it's not all fruit-syrup smiles and sticky fingers, you know. For women with sharp wits and a lively imagination, it's apparently quite easy to disguise poison in berries and pastries or weaponize a rival's citrus allergy – so wicked fae and devilish demons beware.

As any sensible queen will tell you, a good pudding does more than satisfy a sweet tooth. It lets you play with aroma, flavour and texture to create an impression more enduring than a vampire's grudge. It says it's time to linger and relax, and eat solely for pleasure – which is frankly the most magical way to eat.

The plentiful treats in this section are all you need for a mouthwatering feast finale or a moment of cosy romancing.

DA'NEER SPICED HONEYDEW SALAD

This zesty combination of sweet summer fruit and aromatic spices is deliciously refreshing with a spicy kick – you'll never think of fruit salad the same way again. Serve with Greek yogurt or fresh cream for truly princely pudding.

Serves 6

Preparation time 15 minutes | Cooking time 5 minutes

1 vanilla pod (vanilla bean)
175 ml (6 fl oz) water
2½ tablespoons caster (superfine) sugar
1 small hot red chilli (chili), halved and deseeded
½ honeydew melon, deseeded
4 clementines
2 peaches
75 g (3 oz) blueberries

Use the tip of a small, sharp knife to score the vanilla pod (vanilla bean) lengthways through to the centre. Put the measurement water and sugar in a saucepan and heat gently until the sugar has dissolved. Add the vanilla pod and chilli (chili) and heat gently for a further 2 minutes.

Remove the pan from the heat and leave to cool while you prepare the fruit. Cut the melon flesh into small chunks, removing and discarding the skin. Remove the peel from the clementines and slice the flesh. Stone (pit) and slice the peaches.

Put the prepared fruit and blueberries into a serving dish and mix together, then pour over the warm syrup, Serve immediately decorated with the chilli and half a vanilla pod (discard just before eating), or cover and chill until ready to serve.

FAE MOONMILK PUDDING

It takes time to make this creamy rice pudding, but you'll be rewarded with a fragrant bowl of sweet indulgence – the kind of grounding, soul-mending food that friendly fae like to offer. Serve in warm bowls by the fire, or dress with honey, nuts and fruit for a fine end to a fantastical feast.

Serves 4–6

Preparation time 5 minutes | Cooking time 50 minutes

- 1 litre (1¾ pints) milk
- 250 ml (8 fl oz) double (heavy) cream
- 100 g (3½ oz) caster (superfine) sugar
- 1 cinnamon stick
- pared rind of ½ lemon, cut into strips
- 200 g (7 oz) pudding or risotto rice
- 2 egg yolks, beaten
- ground cinnamon, for sprinkling (optional)

Place the milk, cream, sugar, cinnamon stick and lemon rind in a large saucepan and bring to the boil. Add the rice, stir well and reduce the heat to low. Cook for 45 minutes, stirring occasionally, until most of the liquid has been absorbed and the rice is very tender.

Stir a spoonful of the liquid into the beaten egg yolks, then pour the egg mixture into the pan and cook for a further 1 minute until the pudding is creamy. Remove the cinnamon stick and lemon rind.

Serve warm or chilled, sprinkled with a little ground cinnamon, if liked.

For caramelized rice puddings, make the rice pudding as above. Spoon into 4 ramekins and leave to cool slightly. Sprinkle 1 tablespoon caster (superfine) sugar over the top of each pudding, making sure the tops are covered. Caramelize the tops using a blowtorch or place under a preheated hot grill (broiler) for 1–2 minutes until the sugar browns and melts.

ORANGE CARAMEL NEMESIS FLANS

With zesty orange and bitter-sweet caramel flavours, these luxurious puddings are intensely aromatic and silky smooth on the tongue. Oranges might be Jack Barlowe's downfall in Basgiath, but what a way to go! Serve with whipped cream and dressed with orange-rind curls and rose petals for a flamboyant final course.

Serves 4
Preparation time 15 minutes, plus cooling and chilling
Cooking time 35 minutes

- finely grated zest and juice of 5 large oranges
- 250 g (8 oz) caster (superfine) sugar
- 1 tablespoon cornflour (cornstarch)
- 6 eggs
- 3 egg yolks

FOR THE CARAMEL

- 75 g (3 oz) caster (superfine) sugar
- 5 tablespoons water

Make the caramel. Place the sugar and measurement water in a saucepan and cook over a low heat until the sugar has dissolved. Increase the heat and cook until it is a caramel colour. Divide between 4 dariole moulds, coating the bases and a little up the sides.

Place the orange zest, 400 ml (14 fl oz) of the orange juice and the sugar in a saucepan and cook over a low heat until the sugar has dissolved. Mix the cornflour (cornstarch) with 2 tablespoons of the remaining orange juice (or water), then stir into the pan and cook for 2 minutes until thickened.

Pass through a fine sieve (strainer) and leave to cool slightly. Beat the eggs and egg yolks in a large bowl, then stir in the orange mixture, a little at a time. Spoon into the prepared moulds, place in a roasting tin and pour in boiling water to come two-thirds up the sides of the moulds.

Bake in a preheated oven, 150°C (300°F), Gas Mark 2, for 20–25 minutes until just set with a slight wobble in the centres. Leave to cool, then chill for at least 2 hours or overnight. Turn out on to serving plates and serve.

Wine & Honey-Baked Figs

Nothing says temptation like sweet, plump figs baked in wine and dripping with honey. Serve yours with yogurt or crème fraîche for a divine dessert.

Serves 4

Preparation time 5 minutes | Cooking time 15–20 minutes

250 ml (8 fl oz) fruity red wine, such as Rioja
3 tablespoons soft brown sugar
3 tablespoons clear honey
1 cinnamon stick
12 small figs
25 g (1 oz) butter
yogurt or crème fraîche, to serve

Place the wine, sugar, honey and cinnamon stick in a saucepan and simmer until the sugar has dissolved. Cut a small cross down into the top of each fig using a sharp knife, then place in a greased baking dish. Pour the wine mixture over each fig and top each with a little of the butter.

Bake in a preheated oven, 200°C (400°F), Gas Mark 6, for 10–15 minutes until the figs are soft. Serve with yogurt or crème fraîche and the sauce drizzled over.

MAGNUS BANE'S FROZEN BELLINIS

Simple, sweet, fruity and refreshing, these frozen bellinis have the kind of *Shadowhunters* sparkle Brooklyn's glamorous High Warlock deserves. Serve in tall, frosted glasses with long spoons to make the most of their beauty.

Serves 4
Preparation time 15 minutes

750 g (1½ lb) ripe peaches, stoned (pitted)
100 ml (3½ fl oz) sweet sparkling wine
juice of ½ lemon
1 tablespoon icing (confectioners') sugar, plus extra to taste
15 ice cubes

Put 500 g (1 lb) of the peaches in a blender and blend to a purée. Transfer to a large bowl. Slice the remaining fruit, put in a separate bowl and gently toss with the wine.

Whizz the lemon juice, icing (confectioners') sugar and ice cubes in the blender until the ice is well crushed – you may need to do this in stages to avoid overheating the blender. Transfer the crushed ice mixture to the bowl with the fruit and stir well to combine thoroughly.

Taste, adding more icing sugar if necessary. Spoon into 4 glasses and serve immediately, topped with the sliced fruit.

APOLLYON BAKLAVA

A decadent, rich treat full of sunfire magic for sticky pleasure, this citrus baklava has a lighter flavour than traditional baklava but keeps the rich, crisp, buttery layers. Eat as it is, or up the ante with pistachio ice cream.

Makes 24
Preparation time 30 minutes, plus chilling
Cooking time 35–40 minutes

400 g (13 oz) ready-made filo pastry (phyllo dough), defrosted if frozen
125 g (4 oz) butter, melted
few slivers of pistachio nuts, to decorate

FOR THE FILLING
100 g (3½ oz) walnut pieces
100 g (3½ oz) shelled pistachio nuts
100 g (3½ oz) blanched almonds
75 g (3 oz) caster (superfine) sugar
½ teaspoon ground cinnamon

FOR THE SYRUP
1 lemon
1 small orange
250 g (8 oz) caster (superfine) sugar
pinch of ground cinnamon
150 ml (¼ pint) water

Make the filling. Dry-fry the nuts in a nonstick pan (skillet) for 3–4 minutes, stirring until lightly browned. Leave to cool slightly then roughly chop and mix with the sugar and spice.

Unfold the pastry (dough) and cut it into rectangles the same size as the base of an 18 x 28 cm (7 x 11 inch) small roasting tin.

Wrap half the pastry in clingfilm (plastic wrap) so that it doesn't dry out. Brush each unwrapped sheet of pastry with melted butter then layer up in the roasting tin. Spoon in the nut mixture then unwrap and cover with the remaining pastry, buttering layers as you go. Cut the pastry into 6 squares, then cut each square into 4 triangles.

Bake in a preheated oven, 180°C (350°F), Gas Mark 4, for 30–35 minutes, covering with foil after 20 minutes to prevent it overbrowning.

Meanwhile, make the syrup. Pare the rind off the citrus fruit with a zester or vegetable peeler then cut the rind into strips. Squeeze the juice. Put the strips and juice in a saucepan with the sugar, cinnamon and measurement water. Heat gently until the sugar dissolves then simmer for 5 minutes without stirring.

Pour the hot syrup over the pastry as soon as it comes out of the oven. Leave to cool, then chill for 3 hours. Remove from the tin and arrange the pieces on a serving plate, sprinkled with slivers of pistachio.

You can store baklava in the refrigerator for up to 2 days.

MIDNIGHT PARTY CINNAMON & PECAN THINGS

These pillowy, sweet cinnamon rolls are as fantastically delicious as you'd find at *Le Cirque des Rêves*, with pecans for a surprise nutty crunch. Serve warm and gooey from the oven to the smell of comfort, or cold for a denser texture.

Makes 10
Preparation time 45 minutes, plus standing and proving
Cooking time 30 minutes

1 tablespoon ground flaxseed
200 ml (7 fl oz) almond milk
15 g (½ oz) fast-action dried yeast
450 g (14½ oz) strong white bread flour, plus extra for dusting
½ teaspoon salt
75 g (3 oz) butter, softened and cubed
50 g (2 oz) soft light brown sugar
125 g (4 oz) icing (confectioners') sugar
sunflower oil, for oiling

FOR THE FILLING
100 g (4 oz) butter, softened
8 tablespoons soft light brown sugar
2 teaspoons ground cinnamon
75 g (3 oz) pecan nuts, roughly chopped
6 fresh Medjool dates, stoned (pitted) and mashed
2 tablespoons maple syrup

Mix the flaxseed with 3 tablespoons of water and set aside. Heat the milk gently in a saucepan until lukewarm, then stir in the yeast and leave to stand for 10 minutes.

Mix the flour and salt in a large bowl, add the butter and combine until the mixture resembles breadcrumbs, then stir in the brown sugar. Combine the flaxseed and yeast mixtures together, then stir into the flour mixture to make a smooth, soft dough. Tip the dough onto a lightly floured surface and knead for about 5 minutes until smooth and elastic. Put it in a clean bowl, cover with clingfilm (plastic wrap) and leave to rise in a warm place for 10 minutes.

Make the filling. Mix the butter, sugar and cinnamon in a bowl until well combined, then add the pecans, dates and maple syrup.

Turn the dough onto a lightly floured surface and knead for 2 minutes until smooth. Roll out to a rectangle about 30 x 45 cm (12 x 18 inches). Spread the filling evenly across it, then roll tightly from one of the longer sides to form a spiral. Slice into 10 even slices, then place well spaced on a baking sheet, cover loosely with lightly oiled clingfilm and leave to prove in a warm place for 30 minutes.

Remove the clingfilm and bake in a preheated oven, 200°C (400°F), Gas Mark 6, for 25 minutes until golden. Leave to cool on a wire rack.

Put the icing (confectioners') sugar in a bowl, add 2 tablespoons of water, mix until soft and smooth. Drizzle over the cooled buns and leave to set before serving, unless you prefer them sticky and warm.

Xaden's Favourite Chocolate Cake

This chocolate devil's food cake is rich, moist and indulgent, with smooth, soft layers that are almost as dark and brooding as Xaden himself – a perfect treat for rooftop romancing. Serve as it is, or slathered in fresh whipped cream.

Serves 12

Preparation time 30 minutes, plus cooling | Cooking time 35 minutes

- 225 g (7½ oz) plain (all-purpose) flour
- 1 teaspoon bicarbonate of soda (baking soda)
- 50 g (2 oz) cocoa powder
- 125 g (4 oz) butter
- 250 g (8 oz) light muscovado (brown) sugar
- 3 eggs
- 250 ml (8 fl oz) milk
- 1 tablespoon lemon juice

FOR THE FROSTING

- 175 g (6 oz) plain dark chocolate
- 75 g (3 oz) milk chocolate
- 3 tablespoons golden caster (superfine) sugar
- 300 ml (½ pint) soured cream

Sift together the flour, bicarbonate of soda (baking soda) and cocoa powder. Cream together the butter and half the sugar until soft and fluffy. Gradually whisk in the eggs, then whisk in the rest of the sugar. Mix the milk with the lemon juice to sour it, then fold into the flour mixture until smoothly combined.

Grease 2 cake tins (cake pans), 20 cm (8 inch) in diameter, and line the bases with nonstick baking paper (parchment paper). Spoon the mixture equally into the prepared tins and level over the surface of both.

Bake in a preheated oven, 180°C (350°F), Gas Mark 4, for 30 minutes until risen, springy to the touch and shrinking away from the edges of the tin. Cool in the tins for 10 minutes, then upturn the cakes on to a wire rack to cool.

Break the dark and milk chocolate into pieces and put them in a heatproof bowl. Rest the bowl over a saucepan one-third full of water, making sure the base of the bowl cannot come in contact with the water. Melt the chocolate without stirring, then remove from the heat and whisk in the sugar and soured cream to make the frosting.

Slice each cake in half horizontally to make 4 layers. Put one layer on the serving dish and spread with one-quarter of the frosting. Top with another cake layer, then some more frosting. Continue layering cake and frosting, ending with frosting on top.

FIRST RIDER FIREBITES

Elite dragonriders and book-club friends alike will appreciate the spicy warmth of these buttery-sweet and crumbly chilli and cardamon biscuits. Pile them on a plate and watch them disappear.

Makes 24

Preparation time 15 minutes | Cooking time 10–12 minutes

10 cardamom pods
2 egg whites
2 teaspoons cornflour (cornstarch)
½ teaspoon hot chilli powder (ground chili)
125 g (4 oz) caster (superfine) sugar
75 g (3 oz) ground almonds (almond meal)

Grease and line a large baking sheet with nonstick baking paper (parchment paper). Crush the cardamom pods using a pestle and mortar to release the seeds. Remove the shells and crush the seeds until fairly finely ground.

Whisk the egg whites in a thoroughly clean bowl until peaking. Sift the cornflour (cornstarch) and chilli powder (ground chili) into the bowl and sprinkle in the crushed cardamom. Add the sugar and ground almonds (almond meal) and gently fold the ingredients together to make a sticky paste.

Place in a piping bag fitted with a 1 cm (½ inch) plain nozzle and pipe fingers, 5 cm (2 inches) long, onto the baking sheet, spacing them slightly apart. Bake in a preheated oven, 180°C (350°F), Gas Mark 4, for 10–12 minutes until crisp and pale golden.

Transfer to a wire rack to cool.

MOLTEN-ROCK BISCOTTI

With nutty-sweet flavours and a classic firm, dry texture, these pistachio and pine nut biscotti are just the sort of comforting bite you want after a hard day or grieving for a hundred years. Serve with creamy coffee, or crumbled over ice cream as a dessert.

Makes 50
Preparation time 20 minutes, plus cooling
Cooking time 50 minutes–1 hour

175 g (6 oz) shelled pistachio nuts
2 tablespoons pine nuts
125 g (4 oz) unsalted butter, softened, plus extra for greasing
200 g (7 oz) granulated sugar
2 eggs, beaten
finely grated zest of 1 lemon
1 tablespoon Amaretto di Saronno
about 375 g (12 oz) plain (all-purpose) flour, plus extra for dusting
1½ teaspoons baking powder
½ teaspoon salt
75 g (3 oz) coarse polenta

Spread the pistachios and pine nuts out on a baking sheet and toast in a preheated oven, 160°C (325°F), Gas Mark 3, for 5–10 minutes until golden. Remove the nuts and leave to cool but leave the oven on.

Beat the butter and sugar together in a large bowl until just mixed, then beat in the eggs, lemon zest and Amaretto. Sift the flour, baking powder and salt together into a separate bowl, then stir into the butter mixture with the polenta. Stir in the toasted pistachios and pine nuts.

Turn the dough out on to a floured work surface and knead until smooth, working in a little more flour if too sticky. Divide into quarters and roll each quarter into a sausage 5 cm (2 inches) long and 1.5 cm (¾ inch) thick. Flatten slightly.

Place on 2 greased baking sheets and bake in the oven for about 35 minutes until just golden around the edges. Leave to cool slightly, then cut on the diagonal into 1 cm (½ inch) thick slices. Place, cut side down, on the baking sheets and bake for a further 10–15 minutes until golden brown and crisp, being careful not to burn. Transfer to a wire rack to cool.

MATING BOND BISCUITS

Whilst some couples plan lavish mating ceremonies, others are happy to seal their bond with the offer, and acceptance, of a stale biscuit. These delicious biscotti are the perfect tea-time treat to share.

Serves 4
Preparation time 10 minutes, plus cooling
Cooking time 15–20 minutes

- 110 g (3¾ oz) caster (superfine) sugar
- 110 g (3¾ oz) plain (all-purpose) flour, plus extra for dusting
- 1 teaspoon baking powder
- grated zest of 1 lemon
- 50 g (2 oz) blanched almonds
- 15 g (½ oz) dried cranberries
- 1 egg, beaten

Place all of the ingredients in a bowl and, using your hands, bring them together to make a stiff dough.

Turn out on to a floured work surface and roll into a sausage shape about 28 cm (11 inches) long. Place on a baking sheet and bake in a preheated oven, 220°C (425°F), Gas Mark 7, for 15 minutes.

Remove from the oven, leave to cool for 2–3 minutes and then cut on the diagonal into 1 cm (½ inch) thick slices.

Lay the biscotti flat on the baking sheet, return to the oven and cook for a further 2–3 minutes to crisp.

Leave to cool on a wire rack.

NEVERNIGHT RED VELVET CUPCAKES

These deep-red chocolatey cupcakes are wickedly moist and darkly delicious – all bets are off, because having just one is an impossible task. For a party spread, arrange them on a large plate scattered with edible rose petals.

Makes 16

Preparation time 20 minutes, plus cooling | Cooking time 10 minutes

- 100 g (3½ oz) self-raising (self-rising) flour
- 2 teaspoons cocoa powder
- 50 g (2 oz) golden caster (superfine) sugar
- 1 small raw beetroot (beet), trimmed, peeled and coarsely grated
- 2 tablespoons vegetable oil
- 1 egg
- 50 ml (2 fl oz) buttermilk
- 1 teaspoon vinegar
- small rose petals, to decorate

FOR THE FROSTING

- 100 g (3½ oz) cream cheese
- 50 g (2 oz) unsalted butter, softened
- 1 teaspoon vanilla bean paste
- 100 g (3½ oz) icing (confectioners') sugar, sifted

Line a 16-section cupcake tray with paper cupcake cases.

Sift the flour and cocoa powder into a bowl. Stir in the sugar. Put the beetroot, oil and egg in a food processor or blender and blend to make a smooth purée. Briefly blend in the buttermilk and vinegar. Add to the dry ingredients. Using a large metal spoon, stir the ingredients together until combined.

Divide among the cases. Bake in a preheated oven, 180°C (350°F), Gas Mark 4, for 10 minutes, or until risen and just firm. Leave in the cases for 2 minutes, then transfer to a wire rack to cool completely.

Make the frosting by beating together the cream cheese, butter, vanilla bean paste and icing (confectioners') sugar until smooth and creamy. Place in a piping bag with a small star nozzle and pipe swirls on top of each cake. Decorate with the edible rose petals.

FANTASY FEASTS & BOOK-CLUB BANQUETS

Whether we're contemplating which court we belong to or the meaning of providence cards, choosing between clairvoyancy and essence tasting, or designing a cute fit for the Summer Solstice ball, it's nice to have our interests *understood.* Autumn Court vibe? Got it. Shadow-daddy energy? Uh-huh. Sharing a common language with others gives us a deep sense of community and belonging, wherever we really are.

We're not just *reading* about riders at Basgiath or Rishan in the House of Night; we're sharing a whole emotional world and imagining ourselves inhabiting it together. Decorating banqueting tables, drawing fantastical maps, creating intricate magic systems or dinky props for cocktails we've designed around dragon personalities...This is how we bring it to life in front of us – how we make imagined worlds real.

If you're hosting a romantasy-themed event, you can lean in to the aesthetic knowing it'll be appreciated – think shadowy book pages, misty roses, medieval vibes... It's about abundance, softness and a bit of drama; slightly undone rather than polished. That goes for the food too. In this section, you'll find what you need for magical snack platters, from tumbles of chunky pies and spicy wings to beautiful homemade bread.

THE 'LIGHT MEAL' CHARCUTERIE BOARD

No romantasy feast would be complete without the go-to light meal that is, essentially, a luxuriously inviting charcuterie board. Choose a selection of 3–5 'cubes of yumminess', or cheeses, with different textures and flavours – for example, a creamy Brie contrasts nicely with a sharp Cheddar; a fresh herby goats' cheese pairs well with a rich fontina; and tangy blue cheese is a must for its boldness. Choose a selection of 2–4 meats with contrasting colours and flavours – for example, wafer-thin ham, bresaola, porchetta and Calabrese.

A pretty pile of fruit, nuts and herbs will give your board the wow factor, adding to the aroma and providing a sweet contrast to the savoury flavours. Include pickles, Bogsberry Preserve (see page 26) or clear honey for drizzling. Add artisanal crackers, Dragon-Eggs Picos Breadsticks (see page 134) or Autumn Court Focaccia (see page 132) for a truly royal spread. Up the aesthetic with edible flowers.

Allow about 56–85 g (2–3 oz) of cheese per person and 56–85 g (2–3 oz) of meat per person

3–5 cheeses
2–4 meats
1 punnet fresh berries, such as strawberries, blueberries, or blackberries
1 punnet grapes
mixed nuts, such as almonds and hazelnuts
a few sprigs of fresh herbs, such as rosemary or thyme
artisanal crackers, breadsticks or bread
edible flower petals

Remove all packaging from cheeses, meats, crackers, fruit and nuts. Arrange crackers, breadsticks and bread on small plates. Place nuts and berries in ramekins or small bowls. Fold, cut and scatter your ingredients across a large wooden or slate board, creating different shapes and patterns around your bowls of nuts and berries.

AUTUMN COURT FOCACCIA

Homemade bread is such a welcome touch, so impress your guests with this gorgeous autumnal rustic olive, onion and rosemary focaccia – it's easy to make and ideal for mopping up sauces and piling with cheese.

Serves 6
Preparation time 25 minutes, plus standing and proving
Cooking time 20 minutes

15 g (½ oz) fresh yeast or 1½ teaspoons fast-action dried yeast
large pinch of caster (superfine) sugar
225 ml (7½ fl oz) lukewarm water
350 g (11½ oz) Italian '00' flour or plain (all-purpose) flour, plus extra for dusting
½ teaspoon salt
olive oil, for oiling and drizzling
1 onion, thinly sliced
50 g (2 oz) pitted black olives
3 rosemary sprigs, leaves only
coarse sea salt, for sprinkling

Dissolve the yeast in a bowl with the sugar, water and half the flour. Cover with a moist cloth and leave to stand in a warm place for 15 minutes until foamy. Stir the salt into the remaining flour, then tip into the yeast mixture. Stir with one hand to form a moist dough. Knead on a floured work surface for 10 minutes until smooth and elastic. It should be very soft and slightly sticky. If too sticky to handle, add a little more flour.

Put in an oiled bowl, cover with a moist cloth and leave to rise in a warm place for 1 hour, or until doubled in size.

Gently knead half the onion and olives into the dough. Transfer to a lightly oiled rectangular baking tray (baking sheet), about 20 x 30 cm (8 x 12 inches), stretching it to fill the tray. Cover with a moist cloth and leave to rise in a warm place for 30 minutes.

Make deep dimples on the surface with your finger. Scatter with the rosemary and remaining onion and olives and drizzle with oil. Cover again and leave to rise for 15 minutes. Sprinkle the top of the focaccia with coarse sea salt. Bake in a preheated oven, 200°C (400°F), Gas Mark 6, for 20 minutes.

The bread is ready when the base sounds hollow when tapped. If not, bake for a further 5 minutes. Turn out on to a wire rack and leave to cool. Eat warm or at room temperature on the same day.

DRAGON-EGG PICOS BREADSTICKS

Picos de pan is a handily egg-shaped tapas staple, with a crunchy texture that is perfect with charcuterie. They're super cute and a doddle to make. Serve piled in a bowl for a dragon-egg aesthetic that tastes great too.

Makes 32
Preparation time 30 minutes, plus proving
Cooking time 10–15 minutes

500 g (1 lb) strong white bread flour, plus extra for dusting
2 teaspoons fast-action dried yeast
2 teaspoons salt
4 tablespoons extra virgin olive oil
325 ml (11 fl oz) warm water
1 egg yolk
sesame seeds, for sprinkling

Place the flour in a large bowl, add the yeast and salt, then stir in the oil and enough of the measurement water to form a firm, sticky dough. Knead the dough for about 5–10 minutes using a dough hook in an electric mixer or on a well-floured surface by hand until smooth and elastic.

Put the dough in a lightly oiled bowl, cover with a tea towel (cloth kitchen towel) and leave to rise in a warm, draught-free place for 1 hour until doubled in size. Knock back the dough, then divide into 2 pieces and roll out each piece into a long, thick rope. Cut each rope into 16 pieces and then roll into balls. Cover loosely with a lightly oiled piece of clingfilm (plastic wrap) and leave to rest for 5 minutes.

Roll each ball into a short log and taper the ends, then place on 2 lightly greased, large baking sheets, leaving a little space between them. Beat together the egg yolk and 1 tablespoon water, then brush a little over the breadsticks and sprinkle over the sesame seeds. Bake in a preheated oven, 200°C (400°F), Gas Mark 6, for 10–15 minutes until golden. Transfer to a wire rack and leave to cool.

WEREWOLF PORK SCRAPS

These juicy pork-belly bites have plenty of rustic charm, along with a mouthwatering sweet fennel and citrus flavour that's sure to please. Tumble on a platter for a 'come eat me' finish.

Serves 6–8

Preparation time 10 minutes | Cooking time 1 hour 20 minutes

3 garlic cloves, crushed
1 tablespoon fennel seeds
finely grated zest of 1 lemon
finely grated zest of ½ orange
1.5 kg (3 lb) boneless pork belly, skin scored
salt and black pepper

Mix together the garlic, fennel seeds and lemon and orange zest in a bowl to make a paste. Rub all over the pork, pressing it into the cuts in the skin. Season well. Place the meat in a roasting tin (roasting pan). Roast in a preheated oven, 220°C (425°F), Gas Mark 7, for 20 minutes.

Reduce the oven temperature to 180°C (350°F), Gas Mark 4, and cook for a further 1 hour until the meat is crisp and cooked through.

Cut the meat into small bite-sized pieces and serve.

THE SHEPHERD KING'S ENDURANCE PIES

The juicy heat of these bite-sized spiced steak pies has a timeless appeal that will keep guests coming back for more. Pile on a wooden board for a warming addition to your medieval feast.

Makes 24

Preparation time 30 minutes, plus chilling | Cooking time 15 minutes

flour, for dusting
470 g (15 oz) ready-made shortcrust pastry (pie crust), defrosted if frozen
beaten egg, to glaze
sifted icing (confectioners') sugar, for dusting

FOR THE FILLING
100 ml (3½ fl oz) brandy
100 g (3½ oz) currants
100 g (3½ oz) raisins
40 g (1½ oz) glacé or stem (crystallised or candied) ginger, chopped
grated zest of ½ orange
grated zest of ½ lemon
½ teaspoon ground mixed spice (apple pie spice)
¼ teaspoon grated nutmeg
50 g (2 oz) blanched almonds, chopped
200 g (7 oz) extra lean minced (ground) beef
100 g (3½ oz) shredded suet
1 tart dessert apple, cored and grated

Make the filling. Pour the brandy into a saucepan, bring just to the boil, then add the dried fruit, ginger, fruit zest and spices and leave to cool. Mix in the almonds, beef, suet and apple, then cover and leave in the refrigerator overnight so that the flavours can develop.

Next day, roll out two-thirds of the pastry (pie crust) on a lightly floured surface and stamp out 7.5 cm (3 inch) circles with a plain biscuit (cookie) cutter. Press into the greased sections of 2 × 12-section muffin trays, rerolling the pastry as needed. Spoon in the filling.

Add any pastry trimmings to the reserved pastry, then roll out and stamp out 24 × 6 cm (2½ inch) plain circles for the pie tops, rerolling the trimmings as needed. Brush the edges of the filled pie bases with beaten egg, add the lids and press the edges together well.

Brush the tops with beaten egg, then make 4 small steam vents. Bake in a preheated oven, 190°C (375°F), Gas Mark 5, for 15 minutes until the pastry is golden. Leave to stand for 10 minutes, then loosen the edges of the pastry and transfer to a wire rack to cool. Just before serving, dust the tops lightly with sifted icing (confectioners') sugar.

RED DEN DRAGON WINGS

With aromatic, smoky flavours, vibrant colour and a fiery kick to rival that of the most hot-tempered type of dragon, these spicy chicken wings are a finger-licking treat. Serve where they can be approached from the left or the front.

Serves 6–8

Preparation time 20 minutes | Cooking time 45 minutes

16 chicken wings, tip ends removed
1 tablespoon olive oil
salt and pepper
lemon wedges, to serve

FOR THE ROMESCO SAUCE
100 g (3½ oz) blanched almonds
3 tablespoons olive oil
2 ready-roasted red (bell) peppers from a jar, drained and chopped
2 garlic cloves, crushed
1 tablespoon sherry vinegar
½ teaspoon sweet smoked paprika
salt and black pepper

Toss the chicken wings together with the oil and season well. Place on a baking sheet and bake in a preheated oven, 200°C (400°F), Gas Mark 6, for 45 minutes until golden and cooked through.

Meanwhile, make the romesco sauce. Place the almonds in a dry frying pan (skillet) and toast for 3–5 minutes, shaking the pan frequently, until lightly browned. Leave to cool slightly, then place in a food processor and pulse until roughly chopped. Add the remaining ingredients and blend together, then season with salt and pepper.

Place the sauce in a serving bowl and serve with the chicken for dipping in and lemon wedges for squeezing over.

DEMON HARISSA ROLLS

Bold and smoky inside with a beautiful golden crust, these scorching-hot harissa sausage rolls are dangerously seductive. Serve in forced proximity to your charcuterie board.

Makes 30
Preparation time 30 minutes | Cooking time 20 minutes

500 g (1 lb) good-quality pork sausage meat
50 g (2 oz) walnut pieces, roughly chopped
5 cm (2 inch) piece fresh root ginger, peeled and coarsely grated
1 teaspoon black peppercorns, roughly crushed
flour, for dusting
500 g (1 lb) ready-made puff pastry, defrosted if frozen
beaten egg, to glaze
3 teaspoons Rich & Spicy harissa (see page 48)
salt

Add the sausage meat, walnuts and ginger to a large bowl, sprinkle over the peppercorns and a little salt, then mix together with a wooden spoon or your hands.

Roll the pastry out thinly on a lightly floured surface and trim to a 30 cm (12 inch) square. Cut the square into 3 strips, 10 cm (4 inches) wide, then brush lightly with beaten egg.

Spread 1 teaspoon of harissa in a band down the centre of each pastry strip, then top each strip with one-third of the sausage meat mixture, spooning into a narrow band. Fold the pastry over the filling and press the edges together well with the flattened tip of a small, sharp knife. Trim the edge to neaten if needed, then slash the top of the strips.

Brush the sausage rolls with beaten egg, then cut each strip into 10 pieces and arrange slightly spaced apart on 2 lightly oiled baking sheets. Cook in a preheated oven, 200°C (400°F), Gas Mark 6, for about 20 minutes until golden and the pastry is well risen.

Transfer to a wire rack then leave to cool for 20 minutes. Serve warm or cold.

GRAVE-DIRT KOFTAS WITH MINTED YOGURT V

You won't summon a vampire with these spicy nut koftas, but you'll enjoy them as an alternative to the classic meaty mouthfuls. Serve with a pure heart to repel trouble.

Serves 4

Preparation time 20 minutes | Cooking time 10 minutes

4 tablespoons vegetable oil
1 onion, chopped
½ teaspoon crushed chilli flakes (red pepper flakes)
2 garlic cloves, roughly chopped
1 tablespoon medium curry paste
425 g (14 oz) can borlotti (cranberry) or cannellini (white kidney) beans, rinsed and drained
125 g (4 oz) ground almonds (almond meal)
75 g (3 oz) salted almonds, chopped
1 small egg
flour, for dusting
salt and black pepper

FOR THE MINTED YOGURT
200 ml (7 fl oz) Greek yogurt
2 tablespoons chopped mint

FOR THE LEMON DRESSING
2 tablespoons vegetable oil
1 tablespoon lemon juice
salt and pepper

Heat 3 tablespoons of the oil in a frying pan (skillet), add the onion and fry for 4 minutes. Add the chilli flakes (red pepper flakes), garlic and curry paste and fry for 1 minute. Transfer to a food processor or blender with the beans, ground almonds (almond meal), salted almonds, egg and a little salt and pepper and process until the mixture starts to bind together.

Using lightly floured hands, take about one-eighth of the mixture and mould it around a metal skewer, forming it into a sausage about 2.5 cm (1 inch) thick. Make 7 more koftas in the same way.

For the minted yogurt, mix together the yogurt and mint in a small serving bowl and season with salt and pepper.

For the lemon dressing, in a separate bowl, mix together 2 tablespoons oil, lemon juice and a little salt and pepper.

Place the koftas on a grill rack and brush with 1 tablespoon of oil. Cook under a preheated moderate grill (broiler) for about 5 minutes until golden, turning once.

Brush the koftas with the lemon dressing and serve drizzled with the yogurt dressing.

Xingyin's Love Triangles V

Thankfully you don't need to choose between an emperor and a prince to enjoy eating these tasty flaky spinach and cheese boureks. Serve on a platter as they are, or drizzled with clear honey – like the *Daughter of the Moon Goddess*, you can keep changing your mind.

Makes 36

Preparation time 30 minutes | Cooking time 15 minutes

400 g (13 oz) frozen spinach, just defrosted
250 g (8 oz) cream cheese
2 garlic cloves, finely chopped
1 egg, beaten
a little grated nutmeg
6 sheets ready-made filo pastry (phyllo dough), 48 × 23 cm (19 × 9 inches), from a 270 g (8¾ oz) pack, defrosted if frozen
100 g (3½ oz) butter, melted
salt and black pepper

Add the spinach to a sieve (strainer) set over a bowl and press out the juices with the back of a spoon. In another bowl, mix the cream cheese, garlic and egg together. Stir in the spinach and season with nutmeg, salt and pepper.

Unfold the pastry (dough) sheets and put one sheet on the work surface with the long edge facing you. Cover the remaining sheets with clingfilm (plastic wrap) so that they don't dry out. Brush the pastry in front of you with a little melted butter, then cut into 6 strips, 7.5 × 23 cm (3 × 9 inches).

Put a teaspoon of the spinach mixture near the bottom right corner of each strip. Holding the bottom right corner of one of the strips, lift and fold up and over diagonally to make a triangular shape to enclose the filling. Fold the bottom left corner straight upwards to make a thicker triangle, then continue folding until you reach the top of the pastry.

Make 5 more boureks, then take a second sheet of pastry and repeat. Continue until all the pastry and filling have been used up. Transfer to a baking sheet and brush with the remaining butter. Bake in a preheated oven, 180°C (350°F), Gas Mark 4, for 15 minutes until golden. Leave to cool slightly, then serve warm or cold.

TAMAR SPICY AUBERGINE HUMMUS (V)

The sweet, warm smokiness of this chilli and aubergine hummus will take you straight back to *Mages of the Wheel* and its Middle Eastern flavours. Serve drizzled with chilli oil and Autum Court Focaccia (see page 132) for dipping.

Serves 4–6
Preparation time 10 minutes, plus cooling
Cooking time 45–50 minutes

1 red (bell) pepper, cored, deseeded and quartered
3 garlic cloves, unpeeled and lightly crushed
1 aubergine (eggplant), cut into large chunks
1 tablespoon chilli (chili) oil, plus extra to serve
½ tablespoon fennel seeds (optional)
400 g (13 oz) can chickpeas (garbanzo bean), rinsed and drained
1 tablespoon tahini
1 teaspoon sesame seeds, lightly toasted
salt and black pepper

Put the pepper, garlic and aubergine in a single layer in a large roasting tin. Drizzle with the chilli (chili) oil and sprinkle with the fennel seeds, if using, and season with salt and pepper. Place in a preheated oven, 190°C (375°F), Gas Mark 5, for 35–40 minutes or until softened and golden.

Remove from the oven and allow to cool. Peel the skins from the garlic cloves and put in a food processor or blender with the roasted vegetables, three-quarters of the chickpeas (garbanzo beans) and the tahini. Blend until almost smooth, season to taste and then spoon into a serving bowl. Sprinkle the hummus with the remaining chickpeas and the sesame seeds and drizzle with 1–2 tablespoons chilli oil.

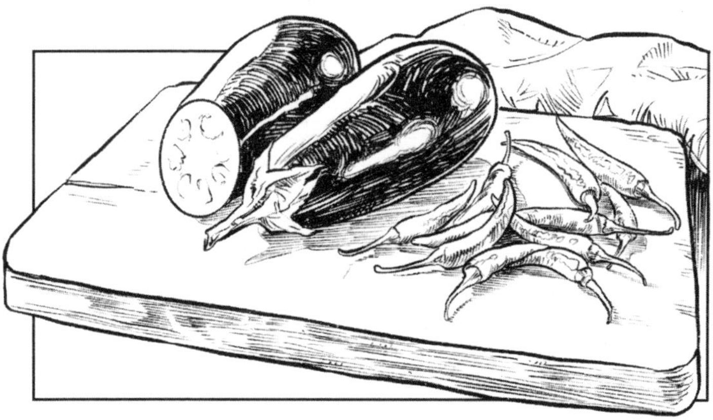

THORNS & ROSES (V)

Give a nod to the court that started it all with this delicious confection. Brave the thorns to harvest your own raspberries and decorate your table with roses for full Calanmai vibes.

Makes 8

Preparation time 10 minutes | Cooking time 20 minutes

2 egg whites
100 g (3½ oz) caster (superfine) sugar
50 g (2 oz) raspberries
4 tablespoons ready-made raspberry coulis, to serve

FOR THE ROSEWATER CREAM

75 g (3 oz) raspberries
1 tablespoon icing (confectioners') sugar
100 ml (3½ fl oz) double (heavy) cream
1 teaspoon rosewater

Make the meringues. Line a large baking sheet with baking paper (parchment paper). In a clean bowl, whisk the egg whites using a hand-held electric whisk until stiff. Add the sugar, 1 tablespoon at a time, whisking well between each addition, until firm and glossy.

Place the raspberries in a bowl and crush with a fork, then lightly fold through the meringue to form a rippled effect. Place 16 small spoonfuls of the mixture on the prepared baking sheet.

Bake in a preheated oven, 180°C (350°F), Gas Mark 4, for 20 minutes until firm on the outside, then leave to cool on a wire rack.

Meanwhile, make the rosewater cream. Place the raspberries in a small bowl with the icing (confectioners') sugar and crush lightly with the back of a fork.

Whip the cream and rosewater with a hand-held electric whisk until it forms soft peaks, then gently fold in the crushed raspberries.

Spread some raspberry cream on the flat surface of a meringue, then sandwich together with another meringue. Repeat with the remaining meringues and cream. Serve the meringues with raspberry coulis.

ENCHANTING ELIXIRS

Romance is a thirsty business. And there's nothing like the backdrop of a brutal interspecies war, a touch of dark magic and a 500-year age gap to get you from 'What a hottie' to 'Scorch me with eternal feral yearning' faster than you can burn a small kingdom by dragonfire.

But whether it's the tavern meads of lowborn folk, courtly spiced wines or refined Ljoslandic tea culture, you can also tell a lot about a person (or a fae, vampire or shapeshifter) by what they drink.

Or can you? It's confusing sometimes, what with all the sleep serums, poisonous potions, enchanted tonics and *many* kinds of blood there are for the taking. Those tempting goblets of intoxicating faerie wine have caused mayhem everywhere from the Unseelie Lands to Elfhame, for a start. And who wouldn't get a feel for boozy hedonism under the constant threat of death while wondering who the enemy really is?

Restorative teas and gentle herbal tonics are perfect for slow-burn devotion or self-care, but perhaps you prefer shared wine by candlelight or a spicy liqueur in your sentient cauldron. In this section you'll find magical mixtures and sparkly sips to share or savour in your own sweet time.

VIOLENCE FIREBALL

Just about punchy enough to honour our favourite Basgiath dragonrider, this cocktail shot will see you fired up and ready for anything. For extra grit, top with cocktail umbrellas in your favourite den colours.

Serves 2 (shot glasses)

25 ml (1 fl oz) absinthe
25 ml (1 fl oz) ice-cold kümmel
25 ml (1 fl oz) Goldschlager

Pour half the absinthe into each glass. Using the back of a bar spoon, slowly float the kümmel over the absinthe to form a layer.

Pour the Goldshlager over the kümmel in the same way and serve.

RED PEARL SANGRIA

It's bold, it's sweet, it's spicy and refreshing – and it's just right for celebrating secret identities and unexpected caresses. Serve with a mask for added mischief.

Serves 10–12 (wine glasses)

ice cubes
2 bottles light Spanish red wine, chilled
125 ml (4 fl oz) brandy
orange, lemon and apple wedges
cinnamon sticks
about 450 ml (¾ pint) chilled lemonade, to top up
lemon slices, to decorate

Put some ice cubes into a very large jug (pitcher). Add the wine, brandy, fruit wedges and one cinnamon stick and stir well.

Top up with lemonade when you are ready to serve, and stir. Serve in glasses decorated with lemon slices and cinnamon sticks.

FAE FIZZ

Like all the best fae, this Champagne and brandy cocktail is perfectly enchanting, with plenty of warmth and sparkle and a light, herbal finish. One is plenty, if you want to avoid disorientation and inhibition.

Serves 2 (highball glasses)

4 mint sprigs, plus extra to decorate
2 tablespoons sugar syrup
crushed ice
50 ml (2 fl oz) brandy
chilled Champagne, to top up

Put 2 mint sprigs and 1 tablespoon sugar syrup into each glass and muddle together.

Fill the glasses with crushed ice, then add the brandy.

Top up with chilled Champagne and stir gently. Decorate with mint sprigs and serve.

THE
CIRCUS OF DREAMS NO-HANGOVER MEAD

Is it an illusion or is it real? Keep your wits about you with this magical fruit juice that looks for all the world like mead. Add sparkling water for a longer, lighter drink.

Serves 1 (highball glass)

1 mango
1 orange
125 g (4 oz) cranberries
100 ml (3½ fl oz) still water
1 teaspoon clear honey
ice cubes (optional)

Peel the mango and remove the stone (pit). Peel the orange and divide the flesh into segments. Juice the cranberries with the mango and orange.

Pour the juice into a glass and stir in the water and honey. Add a couple of ice cubes, if using, and serve immediately.

XADEN'S HEAVEN-SCENT CRUSH

Yes, this really is a smoothie that lets you *taste* Xaden's minty, lemony scent. Drink alone in a darkened room. (Fade to black.)

Serves 1 (highball glass)

250 g (8 oz) cucumber, plus extra to serve (optional)
½ lemon
3–4 fresh mint leaves
2–3 ice cubes

Peel and roughly chop the cucumber. Squeeze the lemon.

Put the cucumber and lemon into a food processor or blender with the mint leaves and ice cubes and process briefly.

Pour the drink into a tall glass, decorate with a strip of cucumber, if liked, and serve immediately.

MOONPLUME MIDNIGHT ELIXIR

Stay well out of sunlight to enjoy this iridescent midnight mocktail with a subtle fiery kick. Top up with sparkling water for a longer, lighter drink.

Makes 200 ml (7 fl oz) (highball glass)

2.5 cm (1 inch) piece fresh root ginger
250 g (8 oz) blueberries
125 g (4 oz) grapefruit
250 g (8 oz) apples
ice cubes (optional)
edible glitter

Peel and roughly chop the ginger. Juice the blueberries, grapefruit and apple with the ginger.

Pour the juice into a glass over ice, if using, and decorate with edible glitter for a luminous moonlit look. Serve immediately.

KINDRED SPIRITS

The ultimate intoxicating elixir for candlelit gatherings, this flamboyant mulled wine makes a flaming centrepiece for your evening gathering of kindred spirits. Serve it in small cups or heatproof wine glasses.

Serves 15–20 (small cups)
Preparation time 5 minutes | Cooking time 25 minutes

2 bottles dry red wine, or 1 bottle red wine and 1 bottle port or Madeira
rind of 1 orange
20 cardamom pods, lightly crushed
2 cinnamon sticks
20 whole cloves
175 g (6 oz) blanched almonds
250 g (8 oz) raisins
250–375 g (8–12 oz) sugar cubes
300 ml (½ pint) Aquavit or brandy

Put the wine or wine and port or Madeira into a saucepan. Tie the orange rind and spices in a piece of muslin and add to the pan. Add the almonds and raisins. Heat at just below boiling point for 25 minutes, stirring occasionally.

Put a wire rack over the pan and put the sugar cubes on it. Warm the Aquavit or brandy and pour it over the sugar cubes to saturate them evenly. Set them alight: they will melt through the wire rack into the wine.

Stir the wine and remove the spice bag. Serve hot, putting a few almonds and raisins in each cup.

BLOOD OF UNKNOWN PROVENANCE

Celebrate all things vampiric with this sweet and fruity mocktail. Go the extra mile and serve shots in small apothecary vials, or top up with sparkling water in a jug marked 'moral ambiguity'.

Serves 8–12 (shot glasses)

3 apples
150 ml (5 fl oz) unsweetened cranberry juice
125 g (4 oz) fresh or frozen blueberries
1 tablespoon powdered psyllium husks (optional)
ice cubes (optional)

Juice the apples. Transfer the apple juice to a food processor or blender, add the cranberry juice, blueberries and powdered psyllium husks, if using, and process.

Pour the juice into shot glasses, or into a glass over ice, if using, and serve immediately.

SHADOW-DADDY SPICY HOT CHOCOLATE

A spicy hot chocolate that's as intensely dark and seductive as your favourite twisted book boyfriend. Serve at twilight with a dash of emotional unavailability.

Serves 4 (big strong mugs)
Preparation time 10 minutes | Cooking time 10 minutes

175 g (6 oz) plain dark chocolate, broken into pieces
1 large pinch of chilli powder (ground chili)
2 tablespoons caster (superfine) sugar
2 large pinches of ground cinnamon
2 vanilla pods (vanilla beans), split lengthways
600 ml (1 pt) milk

FOR THE TOPPING
200 ml (7 fl oz) whipping cream, whipped
grated plain dark chocolate
activated charcoal powder (optional)
whole dried red chillies (chilis) (optional)

Place the chocolate, chilli powder (ground chili), sugar, cinnamon, vanilla pods (vanilla beans) and milk into a pan and heat gently until the chocolate has melted.

Bring to the boil and whisk until the chocolate is very smooth and frothy.

Remove the vanilla pods.

Pour the chocolate into 4 mugs and top with whipped cream and grated chocolate. For a darker and spicier finish, skip the cream, sprinkle with activated charcoal powder and add a dried red chilli (chili) to each mug.

READING LIST

Here is a list of the amazing books, series and fantastical worlds that inspired this collection of irresistible recipes. Have you read them all?

Alchemised by SuLinYu
The Aurelian Cycle series by Rosaria Munda
Blood and Ash series by Jennifer L Armentrout
Blood Orange (*Dracula Duet* series) by Karina Halle
A Court of Thorns and Roses series by Sarah J Maas
Crowns of Nyaxia series by Carissa Broadbent
A Dark and Secret Magic by Wallis Kinney
Daughter of the Moon Goddess (*Celestial Kingdom* duology) by Sue Lynn Tan
Divine Rivals (*Letters of Enchantment* duology) by Rebecca Ross
An Ember in the Ashes series by Sabaa Tahir
Emily Wilde's Encyclopaedia of Faeries by Heather Fawcett
Empyrean series by Rebecca Yarros
Fae & Alchemy series by Callie Hart
Fate and Flame series by K A Tucker
The Folk of the Air series by Holly Black
Hades x Persephone series by Scarlett St Clair
Kingdom of the Wicked trilogy by Kerri Maniscalco
The Kingmaker Chronicles series by Amanda Bouchet
Kiss of Seduction by Rawnie Sabor
Mages of the Wheel series by J D Evans
The Mortal Instruments series (*The Shadowhunter Chronicles*) by Cassandra Clare
The Night Circus by Erin Morgenstern
Our Vicious Oaths by N E Davenport
The Shepherd King duology by Rachel Gillig
Silver in the Wood (*Greenhollow* duology) by Emily Tesh
Swordheart by T Kingfisher
Throne of Glass series by Sarah J Maas
Trial of the Sun Queen (*Artefacts of Ouranos* series) by Nisha J Tuli
Uprooted by Naomi Novik
The Very Secret Society of Irregular Witches by Sangu Mandanna
Vow Forever Night (*To the Cruel Gods* series) by May Sage
When the Moon Hatched (*Moonfall* series) by Sarah A Parker
A Wolf in the Palace by W Style
Zodiac Academy series by Caroline Peckham and Susanne Valenti

PUBLISHER'S NOTE

Standard level spoon measurements are used in all recipes.
1 tablespoon = one 15ml spoon
1 teaspoon = one 5ml spoon

Both imperial and metric measurements have been given in all recipes. Use one set of measurements only and not a mixture of both.

Eggs should be medium unless otherwise stated. The Department of Health advises that eggs should not be consumed raw. It is prudent for more vulnerable people such as pregnant and nursing mothers, invalids, the elderly, babies and young children to avoid uncooked or lightly cooked dishes made with eggs. Once prepared these dishes should be kept refrigerated and used promptly.

Milk should be full fat unless otherwise stated.

Ovens should be preheated to the specific temperature – if using a fan-assisted oven, follow manufacturer's instructions for adjusting the time and the temperature.

This book includes dishes made with nuts and nut derivatives. It is advisable for those with known allergic reactions to nuts and nut derivatives and those who may be potentially vulnerable to these allergies, such as pregnant and nursing mothers, invalids, the elderly, babies and children, to avoid dishes made with nuts and nut oils. It is also prudent to check the labels of preprepared ingredients for the possible inclusion of nut derivatives.

INDEX

RAISING READERS

Books Build Bright Futures

Dear Reader,

We'd love your attention for one more page to tell you about the crisis in children's reading, and what we can all do.

Studies have shown that reading for fun is the single **biggest predictor of a child's future life chances** – more than family circumstance, parents' educational background or income. It improves academic results, mental health, wealth, communication skills, ambition and happiness.[1]

The number of children reading for fun is in rapid decline. Young people have a lot of competition for their time. In 2024, 1 in 10 children and young people in the UK aged 5 to 18 did not own a single book at home.[2]

Hachette works extensively with schools, libraries and literacy charities, but here are some ways we can all raise more readers:

- Reading to children for just 10 minutes a day makes a difference
- Don't give up if children aren't regular readers – there will be books for them!
- Visit bookshops and libraries to get recommendations
- Encourage them to listen to audiobooks
- Support school libraries
- Give books as gifts

There's a lot more information about how to encourage children to read on our website: **www.RaisingReaders.co.uk**

Thank you for reading.

hachette LIVRE

[1] OECD, '21st-Century Readers: Developing Literacy Skills in a Digital World', 2021, https://www.oecd.org/en/publications/21st-century-readers_a83d84cb-en.html

[2] National Literacy Trust, 'Book Ownership in 2024', November 2024, https://literacytrust.org.uk/research-services/research-reports/book-ownership-in-2024